SOULMATE ADDICTION

The Power and Peril of Love's Eternal Bonds

Judith Hartke

Printed in the United States of America
First Printing, 2025
Cover design by Mariah Corrigan

www.SoulmateAddiction.com

To Caelan

May you walk beside the one who speaks the language of your soul.

Contents

Introduction

You would not have called to me unless I had been calling to you, said the Lion.
— C.S. Lewis, The Silver Chair

They say love is a drug, but what happens when your soul provides you with the ultimate addiction?

Welcome to a world where Soulmates and Twin Flames are both the cure and the disease, and where the desire to break free can sometimes feel like a battle for your very soul.

It has been said that these souls are destined to find each other, but that destiny can come at a cost. Soulmate Addiction explores the realm where the addictive qualities of the Soulmate and Twin Flame connection can lead down an intoxicating yet perilous path. Where love knows no bounds, and hearts can intertwine in an irresistible, timeless dance of the sweetest bliss within the most treacherous snare. The allure of this love can prove to be the most dangerous drug of all.

If you are reading this, you may be familiar with the addictive qualities of a Soulmate connection. You may have experienced the strength of those exquisite, otherworldly threads that bind us to certain individuals across lifetimes. You may also have encountered your heart's greatest desire but then found yourself in the most excruciating and inescapable trap of an addiction that threatens your stability and life's chance at happiness.

If so, this book was created with you in mind, for the pain can be conquered, and the path can be cleared for a life of happiness to unfold. Like all addictions, it will take effort, understanding, and a great measure of self-love to find your way back from the shores of Soulmate Addiction, but unlike other addictions, this one was predestined and orchestrated by the Divine, for once lost in this sea, you will never be the same, but then you were never meant to be. Soulmate Addiction can be one of the most painful paths we can experience in our human form, but it also offers one of the greatest transformative platforms from which to grow. Though this is an addiction like no other, it is also a soul-level course of study that bestows on its graduates one of the highest degrees of achievement.

In this book, we will explore the courses offered in this "degree"—from the required class of otherworldly love to the high-powered electives of personal growth and expansion. Those who have experienced this mystical love know that there is so much more going on within these relationships than what we have been led to understand by mainstream relationship and mental health experts. There are many books and resources addressing the topic of "Love Addiction," most of which explore the pitfalls of love and attraction grown wild or obsession springing from unhealed wounds and traumas. Addiction is a serious thing and not to be taken lightly. These afflictions certainly do exist, and those finding themselves in the midst of such an experience might benefit greatly from outside assistance and the deep work of healing their inner landscape.

However, while a main focus of this book is certainly on the addictive aspect of this profound love, it also addresses what so many of these other resources leave out— the simple fact that many of these love connections are addictive because they are not merely a result of trauma, ego, or unhealed wounds. Many of these connections are addictive because they are with Soulmate or Twin Flame partners and, therefore, are built on an intentional, eternal blueprint. To trivialize or ignore these eternal bonds taints these stories with dark qualities of blame when there is so much more to these timeless relationships; Treating them as a failing of the mind when they are truly a connection of the soul does a deep disservice to the people struggling and suffering in the depths of these immortal waters.

So, give yourself a break.

If you've ever felt confused, misunderstood, or embarrassed to share the depth of your Soulmate or Twin Flame journey with even your closest allies, know that you are not alone. This love defies the limits of time and space, an ethereal force that transcends the ordinary and touches the extraordinary, weaving a mystical tapestry across lifetimes. Within these pages, we will explore how such boundless love can shift from blissful ecstasy to agonizing addiction—and what to do when it does. *Soulmate Addiction* will help guide you through this mystical experience, offering support and understanding to those who have felt the inexorable, magnetic pull of their Soulmate's energy, and sharing wisdom for those seeking to navigate the complex, addictive qualities that so often accompany these profound connections. Through stories that bring solace* and tools that aid in healing, this book is for you—the seeker, the lover, the soul entwined in the karmic dance of love and transformation.

I am not a counselor, therapist, or medical doctor. What I am is a person who has spent many years as a spiritual coach, teacher, and intuitive consultant and has touched on thousands of relationships containing these ethereal threads. Through the lens of my own experiences working with people across the globe, in nearly every culture, religion, and economic background, I have found a common pain and a familiar echo in the stories of so many of these love relationships. Soulmates or Twin Flame bonding is not merely a love addiction on steroids. They are karmic connections that defy the logic of the mind and overwhelm the resistance of the heart.

Through my work with countless souls entangled in connections marked by these mystical imprints, I have found that the world of modern psychology offers little solace for those struggling with connections of this magnitude. The existence of these soul connections remains unrecognized, and while emotional addiction can be a very real struggle in these love stories, the eternal nature of these relationships is seldom given the reverence, depth, or consideration it truly deserves. This is not to say that traditional avenues offer no support—on the contrary, I strongly encourage those experiencing Soulmate Addiction to seek help in whatever way feels most aligned and supportive to them.

With a growing awareness of trauma bonding, attachment styles, personality frameworks like the Enneagram and Myers-Briggs, and the lasting impact of childhood wounds, we've made incredible strides in understanding how humans navigate relationships. These insights have deepened our awareness of connection, fostering greater personal growth and more fulfilling partnerships. Yet, despite all this progress, one crucial element is often overlooked: the soul's journey and its deep influence on who we love and why. How is it that seemingly rational people find themselves entangled in relationships that defy logic? Why do some remain endlessly devoted to those who offer little in return? What unseen force binds two souls together against impossible odds, or keeps another longing for a love lost decades ago? While psychology explains patterns, it cannot fully capture the mystical, magnetic pull of soul connections. This is the missing piece—the deeper truth behind the loves that transform us, challenge us, and refuse to let us go.

The influence of Soulmates and Twin Flames has long been the stuff of legend—romanticized, mysterious, and often misunderstood. Yet, for those who experience it, the confusion, intensity, and emotional upheaval are profoundly real. This book is about making sense of that journey, even if only for ourselves. Seeking therapy, tools, and support when needed is essential, but just as important is the reassurance that we are not crazy, and we are not alone. May these pages bring comfort, clarity, and a guiding light—deepening the understanding of the timeless bonds that shape our soul's path.

Now let's get started on a journey through life's sweetest, most transformative, and enigmatic addiction.

Though the basis for the stories in this book is true, names, many details, and identifying characteristics have been changed to add clarity and protect the identities of the individuals included.

CHAPTER 1

SOULMATES AND TWIN FLAMES: DEFINING THE MYSTICAL CONNECTIONS OF THE HEART

What you seek is seeking you. Rumi

The woman on the phone was insistent. She needed clarity—clear, undeniable explanations for her experience and what she was meant to do next. She wasn't particularly spiritual, and years of exhaustion from a demanding career had left her somewhat jaded, with little patience for illusions or speculation. Yet, something had occurred—something she couldn't ignore, explain, or rationalize away, and she was determined to understand what had happened and what it was asking of her.

Dr. Carmen recounted the moment to me in vivid detail. Just the day before, during a routine monthly meeting with over two hundred physicians at a busy city hospital, she had experienced a moment that would change her life forever. In the crowded room filled with colleagues, her eyes had locked with those of an unfamiliar co-worker, and in an instant, a flash of something extraordinary occurred—an experience that defied logic or explanation but was undeniably real.

In that fleeting moment of connection with this unknown man, she had been overcome by a profound sense of familiarity, a rush of safety, and a love so deep and unconditional it took her breath away. It was as if, for that one electric second, she had come home—not to a place, but to a presence. The connection was instantaneous, staggering, and unlike anything she had ever known.

The doctor had never spent much time contemplating past lives, soul connections, or the spiritual nature of existence. Yet, in that pivotal moment when she had looked into this man's eyes, Dr.

Carmen knew that she had been struck by some sort of profound spiritual experience—that something astonishing and otherworldly had just taken place that she felt compelled to understand. It was as if an invisible thread had pulled her toward him, awakening something deep and ancient within her. She knew—without question—that she had to know him. But how? And, more importantly, why?

The challenge lay in the fact that finding him and establishing any sort of connection would be no simple task. She had never met him, didn't know his name, and had no way of tracking him down in the sprawling hospital where they both worked. And even if she did locate him, how could she explain her feelings and experience? What if he hadn't felt anything? (This was entirely possible, given that such connections often begin with one person experiencing something extraordinary while the other remains slower to awaken.) What if he was married? What if he thought she was unbalanced? She had spent years building a career rooted in logic, discipline, and precision. The very idea of risking her reputation for something so intangible, so mystical, was terrifying. And yet, the pull was undeniable. Desperate for clarity, she found her way to me—seeking understanding, guidance, and a path forward. She knew this connection was real. Now, she just needed to figure out what to do about it.

In my work as a spiritual counselor, coach, and psychic medium, I've encountered many remarkable stories of love and connection. But this one would have one of the most unexpected and enchanting conclusions. My work is to translate the energy and information that I receive from my guides to provide clarity, information, support, healing, or whatever is called for in that moment. But sometimes it is not so easy. Sometimes, the information I am asked to pass along makes absolutely no sense to me, feels counterintuitive to the situation at hand, or is something I know will not immediately resonate with my client. So I was a little put off by the advice I received from my guides: *Tell her to join a dating app.*

Ugh. I did not want to say that.

A brilliant, capable physician was seeking guidance on how to connect with a Soulmate she had already met. Who in their right mind would want to hear *Go join a dating app* after experiencing something so extraordinary? It made no sense. No woman who had just locked eyes with the man of her dreams would want to hear that. But my job is not to question the message. My job is to deliver it, no matter how uncomfortable it may be. So, I took a deep breath and told her: *You need to join a dating app.*

Silence. That did not land well. After a pause, she made her disappointment in my skills and "useless" advice abundantly clear. Then she hung up, and I assumed that I would never hear from her again.

But the Universe had other ideas, and the power of these soul connections will not be stopped by the inconvenience of professional expectations, limitations, and a room full of other doctors. About a month later, I received a message that once again made me thank my guides and my faithfulness to their message. It was Dr. Carmen. In desperation, she had finally followed my advice and joined a dating app. Having no idea who she was or where she worked, *guess who was the first man to contact her on the app?*

Soulmates and Twin Flames

Soulmates and Twin Flames are the strangers that we recognize, and if it is for their highest path in this lifetime, they will *always* find their way together regardless of the obstacles. These souls are ancient acquaintances, reuniting in this lifetime to continue a journey that transcends time and space. Beyond any other human experience, meeting our Soulmate or Twin Flame is a rare and life-changing experience that sends us on a mystical journey of both exhilaration and pain.

The spiritual dimension of these relationships cannot be overstated. It's a connection that transcends the physical world, linking two souls on an eternal level. Many belief systems and cultures espouse the idea that Soulmates are cosmically entwined across lifetimes. We are born with a longing for more, and the whisper of this relentless, mystical yearning makes our quest for these connections an enduring pursuit. At the core of this quest is a desire for completeness that extends beyond our physical and emotional selves. These relationships are believed to be the celestial puzzle pieces that fit perfectly into the intricate mosaic of our souls, completing a cosmic picture we can scarcely comprehend.

This is not to say that balanced, healthy people are not "whole" within themselves and longing for someone to complete them. This inner wholeness—where one's sense of self-worth and contentment aren't dependent on external validation or another person—is a foundational aspect of personal growth and emotional well-being. While the need to be filled by something or someone else can be a common yet unhealthy element of the human condition, the Soulmate longing for wholeness is one that lies within each of us, residing in a still, silent whisper emanating from our very Spirit. It's not telling us that we are not enough or not complete. It is telling us that we are more than we ever imagined—that we are a whole, extraordinary part of something beyond our wildest dreams.

Many spiritual traditions teach that all souls emanate from a divine source or universal consciousness. The journey of the soul involves descending into physical existence, experiencing separation, and then returning to the source with newfound wisdom and enlightenment. Speaking at the highest level of perspective, the individuality we are experiencing is an illusion created by the Universe for purposes of experience and expansion.

This means that the energy that we are is the exact same energy as that of a mountain, a car, a flower, or a star. "We are one" literally means that we are not just ourselves but everything else as well. That all is contained within us even as we are part of all. From this highest perspective, our Soulmate or Twin Flame would not feel separate from us because they are also actually us. However, as we came in here to live a life of learning, growth, and expansion, most of us experience life in a human body as one of separateness. We see a rock as a hard, unthinking object completely unlike and separate from us. Though we may experience other people as similar to us in many ways, we normally see them as completely autonomous, separate beings.

As a powerful metaphor for this process, we could speak of "Oneness" as the Great Cosmic Ocean of the Divine, and all levels of existence project from that source into more and more individualized and physically focused expressions. Rivers, streams, and creeks projecting from this eternal ocean are part of the Universal Consciousness but take on the illusion of separateness in greater and greater degrees as they individualize, down to the very rivulet that is our own soul.

As these energy streams become more differentiated and closer to the physical experience, a small number of these aspects of the Great Cosmic Ocean can take on a feel of familiarity to us because they have traveled similar paths over similar ground, over the eons—sharing many of the same experiences, geography, and times in human history, with a similar level of consciousness. Most of us have met members from our soul group. When we do, there is often an instant recognition that transcends physical appearances and societal roles. We experience a deep sense of resonance and understanding, and though we may hail from different backgrounds or generations, we may instantly feel a sense of safety, familiarity, and comfort with this person. Conversations flow effortlessly, and the connection is easily forged on a spiritual and emotional level.

In the presence of our Soulmate, the experience is exponentially more profound.

When we look into their eyes, it's not just the present we feel but a vast continuum of shared experiences, a tapestry of past lives and shared journeys that stretch far back into the mists of time. It's as though we've known this person for eternity. In the presence of a Soulmate, we may feel an overwhelming sense of belonging and comfort even in unfamiliar environments. The connection is often—

but not always— immediate and visceral, like finding the missing piece to our soul's puzzle. It brings the intense feeling of coming home, of discovering a long-lost friend, and of realizing that our souls were destined to meet in this lifetime.

There is often an unparalleled level of security and trust, offering a harmonious and comforting backdrop to the relationship. In this sacred space, we are free to be our truest, most authentic selves, without fear of judgment or rejection. Vulnerability is not a weakness here but a source of strength—a doorway to deeper connection. Here, we can lay bare our deepest fears, insecurities, and desires, knowing that our Soulmate sees and understands us in a way no one else ever has. At its highest expression, this resonance and emotional intimacy foster a timeless sense of safety and acceptance, allowing both individuals to evolve and grow without the fear of losing one another. A Soulmate is not merely a romantic partner, but a kindred spirit—one who speaks the unspoken language of our heart.

At its core, the Soulmate partnership is about realizing the oneness of all souls. While friendships, familial bonds, and romantic partnerships all hold value, Soulmate connections stand as the pinnacle of human relationships because they tap into the deepest knowledge of who we really are. These sacred partnerships teach us that separation is an illusion and that love transcends the limitations of the physical world. In this light, Soulmates are not just romantic partners but soul companions on the journey back to the source of our existence.

An even more intriguing possibility of our soul's expression in this lifetime is that the single rivulet of energy that is "us" may incarnate as a single experience or split into two or more aspects, accelerating its evolution toward higher consciousness. Dividing, the soul follows different paths at the beginning of a trail, allowing each of them the opportunity to embrace panoramic vistas of life from distinct vantage points. Each path unfolds with its own challenges, lessons, and experiences, as its counterparts assume the gender and form most aligned with their intentions for this lifetime. Yet when their paths cross again, there is often an immediate and undeniable recognition—an electric sense of love, security, and familiarity, as if they have finally come home. For in that moment, they are not merely meeting another but gazing into the reflection of their very essence. This partnership is commonly known as our Twin Flame.

The term was first coined by Elizabeth Clare Prophet in the 1970s, who was the author of the book *Soul Mates and Twin Flames*. A fiery union of two halves of the same soul, this connection is often marked by electrifying chemistry and an undeniable magnetism that can be both exhilarating and tumultuous. Unlike the sweet bond of Soulmates, a Twin Flame meeting may actually evoke feelings of fear. This is because Twin flames often appear when we are on the brink of transformation, acting as catalysts for growth.

This relationship often can be an encounter of such soul-stirring magnitude that it feels emotionally and spiritually overwhelming, as it is the most intense and spiritually charged connection one can experience. However, as we long for reunification with our Twin, this deep magnetism is often juxtaposed against some gut-wrenching aspect, behavior, or situation that makes it nearly impossible for the two to remain together. The path pushes us to confront our deepest fears and insecurities, become aware of our own inner fragmentation, and integrate it into a more whole and authentic self. So, while we are inexorably being drawn to each other again and again, we can then find ourselves immersed in a relationship that brings agonizing pain and suffering. Things that disturb us the most often offer us the greatest spiritual growth, so while this journey can be torturous, these relationships also serve as catalysts for incredible evolution and expansion.

This challenges the old, widely held belief that, at the dawn of time, two souls split apart and have been searching for each other ever since—destined to reunite in every lifetime and live happily ever after. In truth, while these souls of a common origin often intend to meet again, their purpose isn't just romantic fulfillment. More often, they come together to spark deep growth, healing, and powerful transformation.

Soulmates and Twin Flames are terms that represent two deeply intertwined concepts in the realm of spiritual connections, yet they bear distinct characteristics that set them apart. Though Soulmate connections are believed to more commonly offer a sense of harmony and support, while Twin Flame connections are known to provide challenging and tumultuous experiences, for purposes of this book, I'll be using the term "Soulmate" more often for ease of understanding and literary flow. For those of us on a Twin Flame journey, however, we can be sure that what is covered in these pages applies as well, as what unites our bonded souls are the shared experiences of the spirit while existing in our bodies in this physical realm. The labels we assign to our relationships can be significant, acting as guideposts that shape our expectations, highlight shared opportunities and challenges, and remind us that we are not alone in this otherworldly experience. Yet, because the root of addiction in these soul connections is often so similar, the insights here are relevant to all relationships founded on a deep soul bond where addiction plays a central role, regardless of the specific label used.

These soul connections were not designed or created on the physical level in this lifetime; rather, they were orchestrated far beyond this material world, and each type of connection offers its own unique lessons and gifts. My perspective embraces this spiritual design, recognizing the sacred nature of these encounters. As we encounter the word "Universe" or "Divine," some of us may wish to substitute "God," "Goddess," "Source," "Higher Power," "The Holy Spirit" or another term that suits —it can be affirming to use the language that best aligns with our own beliefs.

Limerence and Divine Connections

Sublime. Intoxicating. Ethereally blissful. The exploration of what exactly Soulmates and Twin Flames are would not be complete without first discussing the exalted state of Limerence that so many of us experience when the first tendrils of soul connection wrap themselves around our awestruck hearts.

A term first coined by Dorothy Tennov in the 1970s, "Limerence" was described in her book *Love and Limerence* as an experience of being in "an uncontrollable, biologically determined, inherently irrational, and instinct-like reaction." Like living in ultra-high definition, limerence describes the euphoric, obsessive love and extraordinary longing that often hits us when we first connect with our Soulmate or Twin Flame. Like a crush x1000, this state leaves us on fire with the energy of spirit and heart living at its highest state—the magical fairy dust of limerence calls our souls to life and captures our full attention. Our obsessive thirst for reunification with our mate can unravel a lifetime of uncertainty and doubt. We *know* this is our person.

An estimated 50% of us will experience limerence at least once in our lifetime, so many of us well know the sweet intoxication of this mythical, magical feeling. In both classic cases and those marked by a Soulmate connection, initial stages frequently carry a sense of uncertainty or seeming impossibility—a time when we can't be sure how, when, or even if the connection will truly develop. Add to that, our life's circumstances can amplify this doubt, making the path forward feel unclear or impossible and setting the stage for the consuming tension of extreme longing and desire. This stage of ambiguity serves to add jet fuel to already obsessive thoughts and intense yearnings for reunification. As the brain floods with the intoxicating mix of dopamine, endorphins, serotonin, and oxytocin, this cocktail of "happy chemicals' can hijack our common sense and set to flying even the most grounded of natures. It's a state that can turn the most taciturn individual into a lovesick child, drawing us further into the euphoria of this transcendental state as our hearts crave the exhilarating sense of being so vibrantly alive. In Soulmate limerence, our exultant souls fly high on love and rejoice in the finding of each other.

The feeling of "coming home" so endemic to the Soulmate journey adds another layer of nirvana to an experience that defies description for those who have not felt it. Once touched by it, it becomes almost impossible to settle for less. While spending time with most people, we often feel a subtle need to protect our soft underbelly— a reluctance to expose our deepest vulnerabilities and, therefore, risk our very core. As a result, even our most intimate partnerships can have a subtle limitation on the depth of connection—though without comparison, most of us would be none the wiser. With a Soulmate connection, however, tendrils of familiarity flow between us, invisible threads of knowingness that speak directly through our hearts, quietly assuring us that there's no need to guard ourselves; this person is safe; this person is home. In their presence, we're free to release our defenses and find sanctuary in a world that often feels too complex. In this refuge of connection, we feel that we have found our one true, safe space.

It's also at this phase that we begin to discover the magic in our timeless connection—where synchronicities abound, and metaphysical experiences often accompany us on the journey, leading us deeper into our timeless relationship. As we begin to draw emotionally closer to our Soulmate, we experience little "nods from the Universe" —positive signs or encouraging happenings that indicate a forward movement for this relationship—at least in the ethers. While we will explore synchronicities and signs more fully in an upcoming chapter, what matters here is that the magic of life begins to unfold as the dry tinder long dormant in our hearts is set alight.

Although all of this is perfectly normal under the circumstances of meeting our Soulmate or Twin Flame, it is *also the stage at which our addiction can begin to grow from the seeds of our eternal connection.* Soulmate limerence is a state that takes us to our highest vibration—where our souls rejoice, all things seem possible, and stunning synchronicities appear seemingly in our support. Our Soulmate becomes the center of this ethereal vortex, taking us to new, unimaginable heights. It's positively addictive, of course. It is here where knowing ourselves is critical in the path of love, for traumas, unhealed wounds, and unrecognized negative tendencies can quickly lead us into an unhealthy and consuming obsession. Obsessing and fantasizing about the object of our limerence is normal in the early stages of any type of romantic relationship, but in one involving a Soulmate or Twin Flame, the risk of falling into the quicksand of a destructive emotional landscape greatly deepens.

There can also be a painful paradox in this journey of Soulmate love and limerence that we will cover more in later chapters: the soul may recognize its timeless match and cry out for reunification, yet the form that Soulmate takes in this lifetime may still carry profound limitations and risks. It also does not mean that we are "meant to be together" and that the Universe is requiring our joining. As we will soon explore, sometimes our Soulmate journey has purposes other than slaking our desperate thirst for reunification.

To add to the confusion, while the feeling of limerence is rarely lacking for at least one partner in Soulmate or Twin Flame pairs, experiencing the state of limerence *does not automatically guarantee that we have met our Soulmate or Twin Flame, and a lack of limerence does not mean that they are not our Soulmate or Twin Flame!* Confusing, but two people need not carry the seeds of eternal connection to find themselves feeling the pure, childlike bliss of limerence, and in some pairs of Soulmates, one partner may not be attuned to the subtle yet extraordinarily powerful bonds that exist between them. After all, while nearly half of us will encounter limerence in our lives, many will not. And while Soulmate limerence brings with it a layer of connection and experience that is impossible to describe for those who have not yet felt it, a more "typical" case of limerence certainly possesses its own beauty and power.

Regardless of the type of limerence experienced, it has been labeled by some as the extreme version of the "honeymoon" phase of a relationship. Estimated to last up to two or three years, it may be interesting to note that limerence is not limited to romantic partners—it can also be experienced with any type of connection and need not—as some researchers have proposed—tap only into the angst of uncertainty, impossibility, or sexual tension to gather its beautiful power over our hearts.

Many authors and practitioners in modern psychology have painted the term "Limerence" with a darker brush, proposing that it can be the label for a type of mental disorder, but this is a misleading perspective. Some root causes named by researchers include OCD, PTSD, separation anxiety, depression, and, of course, addiction. While these and other mental and emotional factors may certainly play a role in many cases, the research completely leaves out even a whisper of possible soul connections and influences. The existence of Soulmates and Twin Flames is a subject that, at this time, may be difficult for science to prove—but what can't be proven is not inherently false and certainly has been misunderstood. While 90% of the world's population believes in some type of God, 83% believe in a soul, and about 50% believe in reincarnation, the idea of "Soul" has not been considered in the research or treatment of limerence or love addictions.

Though limerence can be difficult to understand for those who have not experienced it, quantum physics may have more answers for us in the coming future. Nobel-prize winning research on entanglement theory is beginning to unravel the mysteries of how two particles can be intimately linked and operating in synch, even though they are billions of light years apart. A change in one affects the other despite the vast distance of separation. In fact, current quantum communications research includes the study of the peculiar ability of physically separated particles to actually communicate with each other. This offers a glimmer of scientific validation to those who have known such a truth for centuries—when two souls have been one, they will vibrate together at the same frequency— and strange, supernatural things may happen as a result.

For those of us deeply attuned to the soul's guiding influence in our journey through the physical world, overlooking its influence is not only a disservice—it renders any path of healing incomplete. Fortunately, the landscape of medical and mental health is shifting to more accurately reflect these deeper soul realities.

As therapists, physicians, and practitioners come to recognize soul influences in their own lives, they quietly become agents of change within a traditionally slow-moving system. This isn't to say that traditional therapy lacks value at this time—on the contrary, it can offer great assistance to those in the throes of Soulmate Addiction. Yet, the most meaningful support in that realm often comes from a therapist or counselor who understands the spiritual dimension of these connections—someone who can hold space for the timeless nature of soul bonds and the enduring imprint they leave on our lives. In addition, while we wait for old systems to catch up, there are a plethora of other tools and resources that can be of assistance. From books on the topic of soul connections to YouTube channels, coaches, and teachers, we are not alone in our journey.

As we journey beyond the initial magic of these soul connections, we step into the deeper mysteries that lie beneath them—those hidden realms where fate, energy, and spirit quietly conspire to bring two souls together. Read on, as we explore the mystical forces that shape these reunions and guide them in their sacred, timeless dance.

Chapter 2

The Role of the Unseen: Fate, Destiny, and Karma

The minute I heard my first love story, I started looking for you, not knowing how blind that was. Lovers don't finally meet somewhere. They're in each other all along. Rumi

The desire for Twin Flame and Soulmate relationships weaves itself through our lives as a profound and relentless yearning. What realm feels so integral to the human experience as Soulmate love? Our desire for this union is a thirst for a connection that transcends time, space, and the boundaries of our ordinary lives. Its allure beckons us with an irresistible pull: These connections aren't just romantic; they are spiritual odysseys.

How these otherworldly connections come about has been an endless romantic and spiritual mystery for mankind. The concept of a divine cosmic blueprint has roots in various spiritual and philosophical traditions. Plato spoke of "anamnesis," the notion that our souls carry memories and knowledge from previous lifetimes, suggesting a predetermined path. Carl Jung explored the concept of synchronicity, where events align in a meaningful way, often suggesting a fascinating hidden order guiding the days of our lives. For thousands of years, poets and philosophers have attempted to unravel the complexities and interplay of fate, destiny, karma, and free will, but the difficulties of the task likely exist far beyond our human capabilities to understand.

What most agree on, however, is that rather than a sequence of random events, our lives unfold along some sort of preordained plan. We are not traveling alone in a meaningless, random expanse of events and happenings solely influenced and created by our thoughts or circumstances, but rather live lives orchestrated by a combination of fascinating yet mysterious influences and forces mostly beyond our vision or control.

The Threads of Fate and Destiny

Let life happen to you. Believe me: life is in the right, always. Rainer Maria Rilke

Fate, the unseen architect of our journeys, has fascinated the human mind for millennia. If destiny is the sailboat with which we chart our course, fate is the river that carries us forward. Flowing along its inscrutable path, fate guides us on a journey full of twists and turns, gentle currents, and tumultuous rapids. Swept upon its relentless current, there is no possibility for our return to prior shores. Fate's ever-changing banks ensure that our lives are continuously unfolding with a rhythm that is beyond our control but presents us with the chance to plumb the timeless depths as we surrender to its magical influence.

In the deep waters of Soulmate meetings, fate takes center stage. The celestial threads of these partnerships draw us together with an unseen gravity that cannot be denied, as the Divine Conductor synchronizes people, timelines, and events to align our souls to meet at just the right moment. We are not doing, we are being done is a concept in the Tao Te Ching that speaks of the Universal life force flowing through the center of our being that can guide us on the path we are meant to travel. Surrendering to this energy is what is meant by "going with the flow" rather than resisting and attempting to force the outcome. As we let go of the illusion of control and move in harmony with the flow of our lives, we will find ourselves where we need to be.

Surrendering to the forces of fate and the Universal life force is not meant as an invitation to merely sit on the couch with our remote control and wait for our lives to arrive. This way of living embraces *allowing* rather than forcing, *observing* rather than resisting, and *trusting* rather than giving in to fear and angst. We continue to act in our best interest, drawn toward what excites and intrigues us—walking through doors that open with ease rather than forcing those that stay closed.

Whether we have met our partner or not, this approach allows divine energy to gracefully guide us toward our true path. By trusting in the flow of life and allowing it to unfold in its own perfect timing, we're granted the freedom to move with the deeper current of our lives. Though we may not know when our mate will arrive, we can still savor the cool breeze on our skin and find joy in each present moment. Rather than postponing our happiness or dwelling in anxious longing, we can immerse ourselves in the beauty of the journey here and now. By releasing our hold on specific outcomes, we free ourselves to live fully, embracing life as it unfolds. In the life-changing book *The Surrender Experiment*, Michael Singer writes, "The Universal plan was always much more expansive than my mind could imagine." Fate is an aspect of the great life force that will bring us more than we could ever have hoped for— *if* we remain open to all of its possibilities.

Destiny, on the other hand, holds the space for us to paint our lives with the colors of our own choosing. Within the framework that fate provides, destiny involves a level of active participation—a process of shaping our own worlds with the choices that we make as fate presents us with opportunities and challenges. We cannot control the winds of change or the choices of others, but we adjust our sails to choose our best course forward.

Mariah was on a mission to find her Soulmate as quickly as possible. She had a plan, and that plan had a schedule. Married by 28, kids by early thirties, retired with the love of her life in a cabin in the woods by 60. That was the plan.

The trouble was that when she finally met him, he was married and with a family of his own.

For years, Mariah worked alongside Travis, enduring the daily ache of his nearness. Despite her resolve to be nothing more than a friend, an excruciating and relentless longing simmered beneath her composed exterior—a burning, otherworldly love that tested the very limits of her endurance. Sometimes, she wished it was possible to tear her heart out just to escape the pain. Yet what made this torment both more agonizing and strangely more bearable was knowing that Travis felt the same. Years ago, at a work party where they'd found themselves alone, their true feelings had spilled out, confessed in a quiet, vulnerable moment. At least Mariah had that—the knowledge that she was not crazy to feel this excruciating, mystical connection. Though they never spoke of it again, Mariah took some comfort in knowing she wasn't alone in her longing; she wasn't imagining this powerful connection. But their shared values—honesty, loyalty, integrity—held them both in check. Travis was devoted to his family, and Mariah would never attempt to disrupt that. And so, with silent understanding, they let the unspoken bond linger in the background, each quietly holding the love that could never be.

Mariah was caught in a long-term, destructive Soulmate Addiction. His nearness brought her unspeakable pain, yet the thought of moving on without him was unimaginable. Time and again, she wondered why the Universe would guide her to her Soulmate only to entangle them in such an impossible situation. If fate had led their paths to cross, wouldn't it ultimately bring them together in a true relationship?

The incredibly difficult answer here is no.

The addictive nature of these connections brings a cascade of challenges that will be explored in later chapters, but the first step in this journey is understanding that our only control lies in our own choices. Much like the parched thirst of one lost in a desert, or the desperate gasp for air while drowning in a storm, the Soulmate bond evokes a longing for union so fierce it consumes. It honors no contracts, respects no boundaries, and recognizes no earthly commitments. These powerful catalysts for change arrive in our life on the currents of fate, but in our hands, we hold influence on the rudder and sails. So, though fate may orchestrate the meeting of our two souls, we still steer the course with our actions and decisions—and do so with control of only our own ship.

In these moments, we need to recognize our own role in the unfolding of our Soulmate story. In this theater of love, we are but one of the two stars of the show, unable to play both parts. We cannot know what divine lessons, agreements, or commitments our Soulmate might have taken on, nor can we decide the outcome of a bond that belongs to more than our own will. While we may imagine stories to explain the choices they make—assigning good karma when they choose us and bad karma when they do not—the truth is, we simply cannot foresee how our karma or theirs is playing out. All we possess is the power to choose our own path, to embrace who we are, and to strive toward who we wish to become. If we choose, we can learn how to truly love without conditions—without expectation, yet still remaining open to the possibility of achieving our very heart's desire. It's also essential to remember that we are always supported by unseen forces, guided by a divine orchestration that will always bring us to our best outcome—if we remain open to it.

For Mariah, time became an ally. With patience and intention, she began to draw upon the tools and resources available to her, gradually softening the once-tormenting intensity of her connection with Travis. Through deep self-reflection and a growing understanding of the timeless soul bond they shared, the searing ache of longing slowly began to fade. In time, she reached a place she could never have imagined in the early days of her emotional entanglement with Travis: the quiet, resolute clarity that—for her—the path of "no contact" was the only way forward. It was not born of bitterness, but of acceptance. She no longer clung to the illusion of control over the future, for she had come to see that such control was never truly hers to hold. What might once have shattered her now felt bearable, even necessary. In choosing distance, she was not closing a door but opening one—to her own healing, her own peace, her own freedom.

Through this surrender, Mariah eventually found herself living and working in town far from Travis, sharing a life with her new love and their two children. She felt at peace with her journey and could look back with wonder at the intricate ways of the Universe. Mariah had come to understand that Soulmate love—and certainly the powerful allure of Soulmate Addiction—was no guarantee that all relationship challenges could be overcome. Now, she was centered, fulfilled, and genuinely happy. Though her Soulmate experience had revealed the depth of eternal love and its addictive allure, surrendering to her journey had allowed her to embrace the timeless wisdom woven into its flow.

While this story may not be what we wish to envision for ourselves at this stage of our Soulmate story, it is but one example of many possible outcomes we may encounter as we move through our Soulmate Addiction story. Fate brings us choices, and destiny invites us to play our hand. In the end, there is no end, for relationships transcend the physical world, and it is there that the true nature of our love resides.

Karma: The Cosmic Balancing Act

Logan gazed out the window, shadows of memory flickering relentlessly through his mind. It was in this very room that he had lost his wife of fifteen years. Though Jennifer had been ill for several years, nothing could have prepared him for the events of that dark winter day—the moment she had suddenly stopped breathing in the midst of a seizure. Desperately, he'd called for help, performing CPR through the twenty agonizing minutes it took for the ambulance to arrive. But once on life support at the hospital, she never regained consciousness, and he never had the chance to tell her how sorry he was, how much he wished he could have saved her.

Time passed, and Logan found himself tending to his new partner as she suffered through a severe bout of Covid. Having just begun to recover himself, he was still unsteady on his feet when he heard her coughing in the other room. Something in the sound sent a chill through him. Alexa, already struggling with asthma, had faced some extra challenges with her breathing, but the sounds he heard now were ominous. As he rushed toward the room where she had been sleeping, Alexa emerged, eyes wide with terror. Hands at her throat, grasping at an airway completely blocked, she struggled in total silence. Blind panic washed over him, merging past and present in a terrible déjà vu. Almost exactly on the same date, in the same room, in nearly the same situation. Inconceivable.

Instinctively, Logan began to perform the Heimlich maneuver, but to no avail. In a last desperate effort, he began striking between her shoulder blades, each blow a plea for a miracle. As Alexa's vision began to close in, Logan delivered one more desperate, forceful attempt, and heard a faint cough as she finally drew in a gasp of life-giving air.

In our Soulmate journey, karma plays a central role. These meetings are planned long before we encounter our beloved, and they are brimming with opportunities and challenges that answer the call of our karma. Betray our love in a past life? In this one, we may have the experience of watching our Soulmate ride off into the sunset with someone else. Sacrifice ourselves in order to save our beloved the last time around? In this one, our Soulmate may be the one who lifts us from a life of great misery. Karma is an enormously complex concept that is often boiled down to "payment for deeds done" in our modern culture. However, it is not simply about balance, nor is it about retribution or reward. It is a natural law of cause and effect—the energetic cycle of creating our own reality by thoughts, intentions, and actions across lifetimes. Like the gradual creation of our own personal software program, we write its code with every thought, intention, or deed. Arrogance, jealousy, and selfishness become the foundation of a flawed operating system, while kindness, honesty, and purposeful effort craft a reality that reflects back to us the beauty of what we have chosen to build.

Karma affects everything and permeates our every waking moment—we are the true heirs to our own karma.

However, this does not mean that we are helpless heroes or victims of past actions and only passively play out our roles. It is impossible to fathom our true karma, and it is not necessary to backtrack and determine exactly how our karma has been shaped in order to change our karmic path. We are never doomed, and by meeting obstacles in this life as opportunities and shifting from identifying with helplessness in the face of difficulty to positive empowerment, thoughts, and actions, we can make dramatic shifts in our karmic paths.

When we reconnect with our Soulmate in this lifetime, our karma serves as an intricate web that weaves the consequences of our actions across lifetimes. Though it acts as an unseen guiding force that intertwines our past, present, and future, we are still ultimately in the driver's seat. By embracing the karmic lessons that surface within the relationship—accepting their presence and surrendering to the opportunities for growth and transformation—they can become a source of true healing on our shared path. Regardless of the direction the physical connection takes, engaging with our shared karma creates unparalleled opportunities for the evolution of our soul. For some Soulmates, overcoming these karmic intentions may lead to a blissful "happily ever after." For others, the bond may serve a purpose for only a season, with both partners parting ways after fulfilling their roles in each other's healing. Conversely, when the opportunity for karmic healing is resisted or remains untapped, the connection can spiral into a cycle of toxicity—marked by repeated reunions and separations—or end altogether, leaving their shared purpose unfulfilled.

Modern culture sometimes speaks of "karmic relationships" as those relationships that exist solely to clear up negative karma and, as a result, bring some sort of retribution, balance, or compensation for past actions. In fact, *all* relationships are karmic. The heat of the moment does not prove the value of the flame—some relationships do exist to balance a great deal of karma, but others may provide a much more subtle avenue for movement forward on our karmic journey.

Beyond the influences of karma, our Soulmate Addiction story is shaped by a tapestry of natural laws and forces—soul contracts, astrological influences, the "Law of Resonance," and countless other elements—all intricately intertwined. These elements weave together in mysterious ways beyond the full grasp of human understanding. Yet, each plays its part, guiding us to the people and experiences that nurture our growth and serve our highest good within this timeless connection.

Soul Contracts and Divine Timing

Soulmate meetings are most often completely unexpected events—one minute we are one person, and then the next, we are forever changed. The shifting of emotional and spiritual tectonic plates slides our world into a completely different landscape, forever altering our terrain—and leaving a panorama that may be recognizable to others who have walked this path but little understood by those who have not. Embracing "the love of our life" involves choice, while an encounter with a Twin Flame or Soulmate does not.

The Universe orchestrates these ethereal meetings for a much greater purpose than our comfort or security, and we cannot plan how, where, or when we will experience such a transformative event. Fate brings our souls together for specific reasons, and the blueprint for our journey is laid out before we incarnate into human form. In his book *Many Lives, Many Masters*, Dr. Brian Weiss explains soul contracts as pre-birth agreements made between souls to help each other grow and evolve through shared experiences in various lifetimes. This often explains why certain relationships feel fated. Weiss emphasizes that these agreements are based on love, even when the relationship involves pain or challenges, and the goal is always mutual learning and the evolution of the soul toward greater understanding, compassion, and forgiveness.

Our soul contracts are profound, for they detail the unique role each soul will play in the other's life. Lasting for a day, a year, a decade, or many lifetimes, these intricate agreements outline the lessons, challenges, and experiences that our souls will undergo during our earthly journeys and are designed to help us reach our greatest potential in this lifetime. Whether it's through love, conflict, or reunion, a soul contract with a Soulmate is about awakening and accelerating our spiritual journey and is meant to help us grow, evolve, and, ultimately, experience love on a deeper level. Like two mirrors facing each other and revealing infinite reflections, our Soulmate contracts help us to behold not only the beauty and brilliance within but also the shadows and scars that require healing. This mirroring effect can be both beautiful and challenging, as it forces us to confront aspects of ourselves we may have ignored or denied.

While Alexa had found her life saved by Logan as she was fighting to breathe, she also had a hand in saving his. In the time following the loss of his wife, Logan had been drowning in a sea of grief, regrets, and self-blame. The anguish of losing his partner in such a traumatic way, compounded by all of the proceeding struggles of supporting her as she became seriously ill, had been physically and emotionally draining. When Alexa unexpectedly entered his life, suddenly, he had hope. He had distraction. And he had love, support, and someone to believe in him. For Logan and Alexa, the impossible happenings, signs, synchronicities, and divine timing led them to each other at a time when—unbeknownst to them—they would both need each other to continue on their journey.

The Role of Lessons, Growth, and Free Will

The philosopher Jean-Paul Sartre once said, "We are our choices," emphasizing the role that free will has in shaping our lives.

For those in Soulmate relationships, these choices often present incredible challenges—testing the ego, reshaping desires, and redefining the very essence of love. While fate orchestrates the initial meeting with our Soulmate and our contracts serve as the blueprint for our journey, what unfolds thereafter rests largely in the realm of our own free will.

In our journey, the choices we make can either nurture our relationships or destroy them. Rather than rigid contracts etched in stone, our connections are more like dynamic agreements—ever-evolving as we navigate the complexities of life. We may choose to cultivate patience, practice compassion, or learn forgiveness. Along the way, we might confront deep-seated fears, heal old wounds, or embrace the vulnerability we once resisted.

Each relationship offers a myriad of challenges and opportunities. Will we rise to meet them, or will we find ourselves repeating the same cycles, resisting the growth they invite? Sometimes, the path of healing and evolution feels too steep, and we might shy away from the discomfort of soul-deep change. Yet, even in these moments, we retain the power to choose our response. The contract between souls is not a cage but a framework—a series of opportunities rather than obligations. We are free to renegotiate as life unfolds, shaping our journey according to what our soul is ready to experience within the structure that fate is bringing us. In this fluid dance, we hold the reins, guided by our willingness to evolve and embrace the growth offered to us.

While we hold the power to choose in countless moments, the deeper energetic currents of existence continue to guide us—propelling us toward new situations, challenges, and opportunities. Not every factor lies within the realm of choice, and life seldom offers a simple, linear path. Our own free will never be enough to complete our story, and our karma cannot be manipulated so as to capture the storybook ending we long for with our love. The future is not fixed. Fate, destiny, and karma are intertwined in a multitude of layers of influence.

This leaves most of us fighting an undercurrent of fear and confusion. The love for our Soulmate can be the deepest emotion and most profound connection we will experience in this lifetime, and leaving that in the hands of the unknown is our greatest challenge. Whether we are longing for our Soulmate to join us, wishing for the healing of an impossible rift, or contemplating with terror the end of a Soulmate journey, we humans are driven by an innate need to understand— and so strive to uncover the forces that shape our lives in the hope of gaining control. Yet, no matter how much we yearn for mastery, complete control remains an illusion.

Perhaps the answers lie in the delicate balance between our earthly choices and the grand design of the cosmos. These connections are shaped by many energetic influences, and focusing solely on one aspect will never reveal the full picture. The wisest action we can take is to *embrace the present as it is* and make the highest choices available to us, rooted in our current understanding and circumstances. Acceptance, paired with conscious choice, becomes our highest and best compass in navigating the complexities of our Soulmate story.

Now let's explore the language of the Universe as it speaks to us through the journey of our Soulmate Addiction.

Chapter 3

Synchronicity, Signs, and Soulmates: Love's Mysterious Threads

I closed my mouth and spoke to you in a hundred silent ways. Rumi

Locking the office door, Haley felt the evening sunshine cast a cool glow on her skin and was reminded that the days of summer were quickly turning to fall. The feeling of change put her in the mood for some comfort food, so she headed to the store on her way home.

It had been another long, yet remarkable day in her work as a transformational coach. She was still riding the quiet high that came from witnessing the courage and depth of personal transformation—something that never failed to move her.

Whether it was Haley's elevated state of mind, her love for the cool, fall-like evening, or the fact that this mood of hers allowed for a high state of free-flowing energy, she would never really know. But six products later, she checked out and headed home. Entering the door with bag in hand, another bag on the counter told her that her Soulmate Max had just been to the grocery store as well. Looking inside to see what his mood had prompted him to buy…. *She saw the exact same six products that she had just purchased!*

In the beautiful, energetic dance of the cosmos, what topic sets our soul on fire as much as the idea of otherworldly love mixed with mystical connection?

Synchronicity

The concept of synchronicity, popularized by Swiss psychologist Carl Jung, suggests that meaningful coincidences occur without any apparent connection. It is the subtle language of the Universe, speaking to us through divine connections that can manifest in beautiful yet startling ways. It's as though the cosmos is leaving breadcrumbs along the path of our lives, guiding us toward the people and circumstances that will touch our souls profoundly. Soulmates and Twin Flames are perhaps the ultimate expression of synchronicity—people whose paths intertwine in a way that defies logic, their souls woven together through the cosmic dance of fate and destiny. They are not just romantic partners; they are kindred spirits who arrive in our lives at precisely the right moment.

Daniel had always carried a torch for Alexandra. While their mutual friends drifted through fleeting love affairs and danced through a constellation of young love's emotions, Daniel held a silent and steadfast devotion for her that never diminished in the years following graduation. Over that time, Daniel tried to nurture the same burning flame for other women, but nothing ever quite seemed to fit, and the depth of soul connection was always absent in anyone else he met.

One day, eager for adventure and a short break from grey routine, Daniel boarded a flight to Thailand from his small-town New York home. Embracing the vibrant tapestry of sounds, smells, and rich culture as he walked down a crowded Thai street, for a brief moment, Daniel allowed himself to believe that he saw Alexandra in the form of a woman approaching him in the distance. In that moment, his heart leapt toward illusion, while his sense of reason pulled it back. As the woman approached, his mind could not, for a second, comprehend what the deepest recesses of his spirit had already known. There was his Alexandra, standing before him half a world from home.

Daniel and Alexandra were engaged shortly thereafter.

Synchronicity weaves its delicate threads throughout the tapestry of our lives, connecting seemingly unrelated events in a manner that defies rational explanation. In this time of great serendipity, there is a grand design at work that often orchestrates the meeting of two souls with a grace and elegance that defies explanation. The Universe has a perfect sense of when we are ready to meet our Soulmate, though we may have to endure heartbreak, learn important life lessons, or grow into our true selves before the stars align and we come face to face with our destiny. Sometimes, love's grand design requires patience and trust in the unfolding of our story.

Carl Jung believed that synchronicities spring from the interconnectedness of the Universe with the individual. We can tap into this mysterious wisdom and guidance by paying attention and considering the meaning behind these instances. For Soulmates, it often begins with subtle signs and whispers, like the first notes of a symphony that will ultimately bring their souls back into harmonious alignment.

As time progresses, these synchronous occurrences and metaphysical experiences may intensify. Our eternally connected souls may find themselves inexplicably drawn to the same places, or our paths might cross in the most unexpected of ways. It's sometimes as if the Universe conspires to guide our steps toward each other, as the elegant hand of fate shepherds us along the trail. The moments of magical synchronicity that arise are meant as signposts and startling reminders that there is a greater plan at work in our lives—one that we may not always understand, but we can choose to embrace. And this is certainly an age where this magical tapestry of unseen energetic connections is vibrantly available to us the more we open ourselves up to it!

Bryan contacted me for assistance on his path through a tumultuous love story. Trapped in the familiar dance of the "runner and chaser" dynamic that so often accompanies timeless soul connections, he was desperate for clarity and a fresh perspective on his painful Soulmate journey.

As we delved into the depths of his spiritual and emotional voyage during our session, I could hear the notes of an otherworldly love song weaving its threads through their journey, and my heart went out to him for the pain that can be inherent in such a deep soul connection. As he described the trajectory of their path together, however, it revealed a tale with a twist. Before their first fateful encounter, Bryan had leased an apartment in a quiet neighborhood at the edge of a very large city. Moving in, he gave no thought to the person who had just moved out and left the space available to him. When destiny eventually brought him face-to-face with his Soulmate, the pieces fell into place, and they discovered that *she had only just moved out of that very same apartment* a few days before he had moved in, leaving it as if it were destined for him all along.

A common thread in these unique relationships, we often find that we've shared spaces, friends, jobs, or other strange and unlikely connections throughout our lives, though not necessarily at the same time. Quantum physics holds hope for someday having a scientific explanation of these occurrences and connections, but for now, it is easy to see these happenings as magical filaments—invisible threads that tie us together before we even meet. It's believed that the Universe sometimes embeds many such meeting opportunities into the pathway of our lives—waiting for just the right moment for two Soulmates to be ready to step into partnership.

As we continue to experience patterns and connections in our relationship with them, we can surrender to the notion that our Soulmates are not just random strangers but intricate pieces of a cosmic puzzle. We are not simply on a path of random chances and hopeful turns—we're part of something greater than ourselves, and our Soulmates are partnered with us in this intricate, magical journey of love.

Though Sean entered my life in a very non-romantic way, I felt something decidedly mystical about our connection from the moment we first spoke on the phone. I won't say that alarm bells were going off, but my intuition had definitely been on high alert upon first hearing his voice.

"I'd like to talk to you about my wife, Indra, who has passed. She was a beautiful soul, and her name had great meaning. Would you like me to share it with you?" "Thank you, but no," I replied. "I am aware of the beautiful meaning behind that name." Sean expressed surprise, as the name was unusual and few people would have had familiarity with that information. I shared with him that just two days earlier, some friends and I had finished creating a video exploring the eternal interconnectedness of all things. In Buddhist tradition, this concept is often referred to as "Indra's Web"—a perfect name, and coincidentally, the very one we had chosen for the project just two days before his call.

After our first conversation, the signals from the Universe continued. In a nod to my belief in the unique yet interconnected perspectives of the world's many religions, I keep a variety of figurines, images, and objects representing a myriad of belief systems in my office. A few minutes before Sean was to stop by one day, I felt compelled to place a beautiful figurine of the Egyptian Goddess Isis next to the chair I knew he would be sitting in. Second-guessing myself and this crazy compulsion, I removed it, then placed it back multiple times before finally giving in to this curious nudging I was feeling.

Sean arrived, and in our time together, I learned a bit more about the strange and difficult road that had brought him to me. Though I felt something was very special about this man, I was not sure it was any intuitive directive to continue our connection, so when he asked me to dinner, I had to pause. Stepping into a relationship with someone who was on such a deep healing journey is not always wise, no matter how exceptional I could see that he was. However, I was also one for following the breadcrumbs that synchronicity sends me, so I agreed.

The Goddess of Healing and Magic in the belief system of ancient Egyptians, one of Isis's most notable feats was resurrecting and healing her mate Osiris after he was killed by his evil brother, and the pieces of his body were strewn throughout Egypt. Turning into a large bird and embarking on a relentless quest to find her eternal love, Isis then sewed his body back together and breathed life into his still form with her magic tears. Revived, their love knew no bounds, and Osiris became the God of the Underworld and a symbol of renewal.

It seemed highly appropriate that the Universe should prompt me to place that statue of Isis next to Sean while he was sharing his story with me that day in my office. I hoped that, in some small way, the symbol placed by his side in our meeting had provided a measure of healing and support on some subtle, unseen level. For a few moments after Sean left, I marveled at the mystery of it and then thought no more about it.

As the time for our dinner neared, I found myself having a few misgivings. I reminded myself that there was something truly unique about Sean, so found myself excited, yet also truly conflicted—afraid I might be making a mistake. Lost in the swirl of my conflicting thoughts, my phone chimed unexpectedly. Glancing down, I saw it was from an old friend I hadn't spoken to in ages—someone entirely unaware of the inner turmoil I was navigating. Out of the blue and for no apparent reason, just moments before I was to leave for my first date with Sean, she had taken the time to send me a stunning image by the artist Susan Seddon-Boulet… *of the Goddess Isis healing her eternal love Osiris!*

Elegance in synchronicity lies not only in the initial meeting of our Soulmate or Twin Flame but also in the journey that follows. Even in challenges that inevitably arise as they always do in any relationship, in opportunities that present themselves, or in compromises that need to be made, synchronicity weaves its magical threads. These moments are a form of divine guidance, and though not always a guarantee of "happily ever after," they are an indication of "happily next." When they arrive in our lives, we can be sure that we are seen, heard, and, most importantly, on the right track vibrationally. Synchronicities lead us to the next level of experience and are a way that the Universe can communicate to us that we need to keep going in the direction of thought, intention, or action that has been in our recent focus. Sending signs, signals, and whispers to our souls of which roads to take, which offerings to embrace, or which burdens to set down, synchronicity helps us to align to our best way of thinking. As we listen and heed these divine cosmic cues, we can relax in knowing that circumstances and guidance are arriving for our highest and best as we continue on our journey.

Wrapped in the beautiful treasure box of synchronicity is a paradox: as much as we crave these moments of serendipity, we cannot orchestrate them. Synchronicities are ethereal, divinely sent messengers – tiny Angels that bring astonishing happenings and messages but vanish like smoke into the air if we try to orchestrate or grasp them. They thrive in the gaps between our agendas and flourish when we're open to the unknown. No matter how meticulously we plan or how desperately we wish for them, synchronicities are elusive and refuse to dance to our command. This might be a tough pill to swallow in our world of instant gratification and meticulous control. We're accustomed to setting goals, making plans, and taking charge of our own destinies. Yet, the beauty and delight of synchronicity lie in its spontaneity—its refusal to conform to our schedules or expectations. To fully experience a synchronistic path, we must learn to let go, surrender to the ebb and flow of life, and allow the Universe to guide us as we walk the beautiful path of Soulmate and Twin Flame partnership.

Signs and Intuition

The world is full of magic things, patiently waiting for our senses to grow sharper.
W. B Yeats

Josh felt lost and confused. His relationship had ended with quiet, agonizing finality as he finally came to accept that his partner would neither confront her inner demons nor offer him the honesty he so deeply craved. Over time, the pain of walking away had become more bearable than the thought of continuing in such an impossible situation. The months that followed were marked by slow, deliberate healing, each step bringing him closer to an unsettling realization: he could not fathom how he had chosen someone so misaligned with his values, and even more troubling, he no longer trusted himself to recognize the right partner should she ever arrive.

If he could no longer trust his own judgment in choosing the most significant person in his life, then who could possibly make that choice for him? No one knew him better than he knew himself, yet even he seemed uncertain of what was truly best for him. A year passed in quiet solitude, with no dating and little social interaction. Then, unexpectedly, Josh met Erica. She was strikingly beautiful, accomplished, and radiated a quiet confidence. Her life appeared balanced, her choices intentional, and she sought a partner to share in mutual love, support, and companionship—the very things Josh yearned for. Slowly, a quiet hope began to stir within him, a tender belief that perhaps, at long last, he had found the partner meant to share his life's journey.

In the still, quiet hours of the night when Erica wasn't by his side, a familiar angst would creep in—the gnawing uncertainty he couldn't shake. Once before, love had felt this perfect, this sure—and yet, that relationship had unraveled under the weight of deception and heartbreak. Now, doubt lingered like a shadow. He remembered a friend's advice: to let go of fear and trust the Universe to show the way. She had told him to ask for a sign—something unmistakable—to confirm that Erica was truly the one. Then, she'd said, he should simply wait, open and unexpecting, for the answer to come.

And so that's what he did.

Instead of asking for a specific sign, Josh chose to release the question into the hands of the Universe, trusting that whatever he needed to know would find its way to him. He hoped for something unmistakable—something that would pierce through his doubt and offer a clear sense of whether his path with Erica was truly the right one.

Sure enough, two days later, when he was driving to work on a soft, beautiful spring morning, he pulled up his favorite podcast. To his mild interest, the topic was Soulmates. A common enough theme, he thought, but his attention sharpened as the story unfolded and the podcaster began describing a man who was having relationship experiences eerily similar to his own. He was mulling over the likelihood of these coincidences when his thoughts were interrupted by a sign he couldn't ignore or even explain away…the story concluded with the Soulmate's name: Erica!

At some point in life, most of us have turned to a higher power for guidance.

Angel numbers, animal visitors, random encounters, unlikely happenings, number patterns, or songs—the Universe can get our attention and guide us in a myriad of ways, but much like synchronicities, signs cannot be demanded, orchestrated, or scheduled (in fact, many of our synchronistic moments are actually signs!).

Signs often appear when we least expect them but most deeply need them. As long as we remain open to possibilities and grounded in our trust in a higher wisdom, the Universe always responds. Even when the answer isn't immediately apparent, it is on its way—sometimes arriving in an instant, other times coming to us days or weeks later, quietly emerging from the stillness of the unseen when the gentle voice of spirit can finally be heard.

Signs can be subtle happenings or shocking events in their bold and unerring perfection. We may notice a name and feel a nudge to reach out, gain sudden clarity from a friend's words that address a lingering challenge, or find ourselves being pulled away from a project only to return later with the ease and flow that had eluded us before. We may open our phone at just the perfect moment for us to see an opportunity that aligns us with what we had been questioning and considering. A stranger may start sharing details of a trip they've recently taken that happens to be the exact same place we have been contemplating traveling to. We may also encounter opportunities that resonate with us or fit perfectly into our lives, which are also signs that we are on the right track. Whether it's a mentor offering invaluable guidance, a friend introducing us to new possibilities, or even a stranger whose words resonate deeply, these encounters are often seen as the Universe's way of providing the resources and connections we need to progress. Most of us have been blessed with these types of magical communications at one time or the other, and the more we strengthen and refine our faith and reliance on help from the other side, the more of it arrives in our lives.

A "miracle journal" can be a helpful friend on this journey of deepening our connection with the Universe. When we write down the moments of synchronicity and later revisit them in black and white, it becomes much harder to dismiss them as mere coincidences. Beyond preserving these experiences, journaling sharpens our awareness of the signs around us and helps us cultivate a unique "language" through which the Universe can communicate. For instance, if we frequently notice patterns like 444 or 1111, we can assign them personal meanings—a gentle nudge, a reassurance, or a guiding whisper to reevaluate our current thinking. Over time, this practice allows us to recognize these signs with greater ease, whether they appear on license plates, clocks, receipts, or in countless other creative ways the Universe chooses to reach out. These moments of connection may feel almost magical, but the real magic appears when we notice, acknowledge, and appreciate the messages, and then allow them to aid us on our journey.

There are an unlimited number of ways that the Universe can communicate with us, but what happens when the signs and signals don't appear, seem unclear, or worse yet, contradict each other? While some doors open with minimal effort, others may remain stubbornly closed no matter how hard we try. Feeling confused about or cut off from guidance just when we need it most can be a lonely place to be and cause us to distrust that the Universe really has our backs. Angst, frustration, or desperation are understandable human emotions when we are in crisis or experiencing extreme lack or confusion, but those emotions are the antithesis of the energetic place we need to be in order to see the signs available to us—or understand those that seem to be sending us in multiple directions. In other words, we need to keep ourselves in the open space of allowing without expectation, asking without demanding, and accepting what is without needing it to be anything else in this moment.

It is the ego's insistent demand for immediate clarity that clouds our perception and becomes the barrier to receiving it—preventing us from recognizing the gifts the Universe is patiently waiting to offer. Patience and surrender are the antidotes when our world is not popping with obvious directional signals. It is when we can find ourselves in the space of allowing communication to flow with the greatest ease and clarity that we will eventually find our clearest path forward.

In addition, when we encounter obstacles on our Soulmate journey, it doesn't always signify a definitive "no." Often, it is the Universe subtly recalibrating the timing of opportunities, gently redirecting our path, or prompting us to rethink our current strategy. When we attempt to force a particular manifestation in our world that might not yet be ready to materialize, we encourage fear and thoughts of scarcity to take the wheel while faith and trust are relegated to the back seat.

Another subtlety to consider is that our powers of manifestation can sometimes weave complexity into the process of asking for signs. In these times of shifting energies and expanding consciousness, many of us are finding that our thoughts manifest with extraordinary speed. When we request a specific sign, we might unwittingly manifest the very object or circumstance we seek, rather than receiving it as a divinely intended guide. While synchronicities are orchestrated by the hand of the Universe, signs can originate from two sources—divine guidance or reflections of our own vibration. In such moments, our inner thoughts and desires may project outward, appearing to offer direction, yet merely echoing our own wishes. Recognizing this possibility allows us to navigate the delicate interplay between manifestation and true guidance with greater discernment, trust, and wisdom.

In one instance, a woman named Sofia sought a sign to guide her heart. After years of fighting both with and for her Soulmate—standing by him through deep struggles with addiction and personal hardship—part of her still hoped their story was not yet over. Yet another part of her, exhausted by the long battle, was ready to step into the role of her own champion and protector.

Choosing a sign that would be possible yet unlikely, Sofia asked to see a Goldfinch if she was meant to stay with her Soulmate. It was her mother's favorite bird, one she had always loved for its vivid color and distinctive song. Because Goldfinches were not common in the area where she lived and worked, it seemed the perfect choice: meaningful, yet not something she was likely to encounter by chance.

A day or two after asking for the sign, Sofia heard a loud thump at her office window. Glancing over to the window, she found herself face-to-face with a male Goldfinch perched upon her second-floor sill, dazed from the collision, yet staring directly into her eyes. Momentarily stunned yet aware, he continued to perch there, staring into her eyes for some time before eventually recovering and flying off. Sofia was shocked. She could not recall ever seeing a Goldfinch at her office—let alone one sitting so close, as if delivering a message straight to her soul.

The very next day, while stretching at her desk, she spun her chair in the opposite direction from where she usually faced. As she leaned back and opened her eyes, she found herself staring directly at a female Goldfinch, clinging awkwardly to the brick wall just outside her window. Had she remained seated in her usual place, she would have missed it entirely. Once again, she was stunned: not one

Goldfinch, but two—male and female, in as many days. What were the chances?

Most of us would assume that was a clear sign for Sofia to stick to her path with her Soulmate Jason. However, the rest of the story is not so simple.

Sofia was also a master manifestor. People and events often showed up in her life shortly after she thought of them, things she needed seemed to arrive shortly after she expressed her desire for them, money seemed to flow in as needed, and doors opened as she walked toward them. She knew that in this magical world of signs, synchronicities, and Soulmates, free will and wisdom also play a role, and discernment is essential. She could not say with certainty whether the Goldfinches had been sent by the Universe—or summoned by the strength of her own mind and heart. In a time of heightened manifestation and deepening spiritual connection, she understood that stumbling blindly after every sign was no longer wisdom. The greater our powers of manifestation, the less reliable the practice of asking for specific signs becomes. True guidance, she realized, must come not only from the outer world of signs, but also from the quiet listening within. So, Sofia moved forward carefully, trusting the Universe to bring her more clarity from sources beyond her own powers of manifestation.

In the realm of Soulmates and Soulmate Addictions, it is also true that signs can be acknowledgments of the deep soul connection while not necessarily being a directive to pursue or continue a relationship with them. To the Universe, love is eternal, and Soulmates remain forever intertwined, regardless of the paths their earthly lives may take. While we may concern ourselves with the practical matters of staying or leaving, pursuing or releasing, the Universe speaks from a higher vantage, acknowledging connection itself rather than the outcomes we fixate upon.

Manifestation can also influence how we experience signs, particularly when we encounter ones that seem contradictory. Receiving a sign that encourages us to stay the course with a

Soulmate can be deeply confusing if, later, another sign appears to suggest it's time to let go. In many cases, this is not a contradiction but a reflection of our own manifesting power: in seeking guidance with divided desires, we may, through the potency of manifestation, call both possibilities into existence. Such contradictions can feel bewildering, yet often they are not contradictions at all. Rather, they reveal the subtle power of our own consciousness at work. At other times, it is simply that each path—whether we choose to stay or to part—holds its own essential lessons, offering growth, deeper love, and transformation in different forms. The Universe is invested in our happiness and well-being, but in a greater sense, it is even more deeply invested in the evolution of our soul. It is this larger unfolding, beyond the immediate outcomes we long for, that quietly steers the journey of our soul's growth.

So, what is one to do? The challenges of interpreting signs do little to diminish the quiet comfort and wonder they offer. Signs remain one of the many subtle ways clarity and support find their way to us—not as rigid directives, but as mirrors reflecting what already stirs within. Their truest meaning often reveals itself when we meet the unknown with an open mind, rather than demanding specific outcomes, and when we surrender the need for certainty, trusting that the Universe is always working gently on our behalf—even when the path ahead remains unclear.

It is in moments of presence, when the heart leans into stillness rather than longing, that signs seem to emerge most clearly—not as commands, but as gentle guidance that often weaves itself through unexpected encounters, unforeseen opportunities, and sudden shifts in circumstance, inviting us to align with a deeper current moving through our lives. When we cultivate patience, listen to the quiet knowing within, and move with discernment and trust, we create an inner compass that naturally draws synchronistic moments and meaningful opportunities into our path. In this space of surrender and wisdom, signs remind us that we are not alone in our Soulmate journey. Trusting this unfolding process ensures that, with time, we will always find ourselves exactly where we're meant to be and in the sacred company of those who are meant to walk beside us.

Quantum Entanglement and Soul Connection

In the world of quantum physics, a fascinating revelation has emerged: when two particles become entangled, they remain intricately connected across vast distances. Changes to one particle ripple instantly through the other, defying the boundaries of space and time. This entanglement signifies an unbreakable connection, bridging any physical distance. Einstein called it "Spooky action at a distance," and the 2022 Nobel Prize was awarded to scientists who delved into new discoveries in this fascinating realm.

Entanglement theory can be seen as the first scientific foray into the realm of interconnectedness and oneness that many spiritual traditions and philosophies have emphasized for eons. Challenging the conventional notion of separation, entanglement theory illustrates how all things in the Universe are intrinsically linked at a fundamental level and speaks of a dance between the microcosm of quantum physics and the macrocosm of spiritual philosophy. Separation is but an illusion, and we are all part of a singular cosmic tapestry.

As science attempts to further unravel the mystery of entanglement through mathematics and experimentation, those of us familiar with the Soulmate bond are very well aware that unseen threads bind us together. Many Soulmates report being able to feel what their partner is feeling, sharing similar dreams, or even knowing their thoughts and what they are going to say before they say it. The connection between these Souls is so limitless that what happens to one in some way energetically affects the other. At a spiritual level, they are well aware of what the other is going through and, in fact, are actually a part of it. Our parallel journeys may very well be inextricably linked by the same mysterious laws that govern the quantum realm—our souls, like particles, are entangled across time and space, leading to the remarkable coincidences, psychic connections, and the longing for "home" that seems to guide us to our beloved, our Soulmate, our home.

Dreams

Out beyond ideas of wrong doing and right doing, there is a field. I will meet you there. Rumi

Dreams can play a pivotal role in the journey of Soulmates. In the astral realm that the masks we wear in waking life dissolve, allowing us to meet soul to soul. The portals of the subconscious open wide, revealing our truest selves in a space where critical minds and judgments cannot rule. Questions, concerns, and constraints disappear in this dreamscape space, and ordinary boundaries of time, space, and reality blur. Unburdened by societal expectations or earthly demands, dreams become a sacred canvas for exploring deeply symbolic and emotionally charged scenarios. Words are unnecessary, for the language of the soul transcends the limitations of speech. Emotions, memories, and unspoken feelings flow freely—the truths that may elude us in waking hours find their voices in our dreams, offering wisdom to guide us in the waking world.

While normal dreams may seem surreal and fragmented, the astral meetings of Soulmates contain an intensity beyond that which we experience in our everyday lives. It's as if our waking world is a myriad of grays, while these nocturnal, astral Soulmate meetings are infused with an energetic light and saturation beyond the palette of the world's greatest painters. Soulmates often find each other in this ethereal manner long before our physical selves even meet, and when they do, these dream encounters can be imbued with a deep sense of recognition, a knowing that defies explanation. Upon waking, our Soulmate encounters may leave us with a heart-rending grief as we adjust to life in the lower plain of our physical life, but it also brings a fullness of heart that can carry us for days or even weeks beyond the experience. Bathed in the light of our soul connection, we are reminded of a timeless truth: whether united or separated in the physical plane, our souls remain intertwined, supporting one another as we navigate the days of our lives.

Jaina had a fulfilling career and was surrounded by many wonderful friends and family, yet she felt lonely much of the time. Being with others was a distraction from the underlying sense that this was not her world, and she was not the same as most of the people she knew. She found it difficult to relate at a deep level to many people in her life, and the intensity of her spiritual isolation skyrocketed after she finally met her Soulmate— who was unavailable and trapped in a disconnected, unhappy relationship and life of his own. The powerful connection that drew them together also served to emphasize the distance that kept them apart, and it also accented the gulf she felt between herself and so many others. Feeling almost at a breaking point one evening, Jaina laid down and cried out to the Universe for relief in her prayers. She was so lonely.

What followed that night was a dream that brought her solace for many years to come. As she slept, she found herself in a circle of familiar souls—faces she knew she would recognize in the waking world as her friends and clients. While she cherished the joy and connection she shared with them, these moments could not truly fill the depth of her aloneness. In the dream, just as she began to grasp the bittersweet reality of once again being within a group yet not truly of it, she sensed a presence beside her. A soul settled next to her, and in an instant, an overwhelming sense of belonging washed over her. She felt safe. Seen. Home. The spiritual sustenance to her starving soul was instantaneous and filled her to overflowing with feelings of love and belonging.

This soul gently took her hand in his, and as her gaze traveled up to the beloved face she had long known in the depths of her being, she recognized him—her Soulmate. In that moment, her spirit was profoundly consoled. The timing was immaculate; the message, perfect. Her loneliness, so deeply rooted, dissolved under the weight of this sacred connection. The Universe had heard her cries and responded with an embrace that nourished her soul. For months and years afterward, the memory of this dream remained a beacon of reassurance, carrying her through the many tides of her life.

When two Soulmates meet in the ethereal realm of dreams, their souls bridge the physical divide, reaching for one another beyond the boundaries of this world, no matter the circumstances of their earthly lives. In the chapters that follow, we will explore more deeply the profound bonds and entanglements that often accompany these mystical connections.

Nothing is as intoxicating as the taste of true oneness. It is the essence we all seek, the nourishment we all need. Beneath the distractions and diversions of the material world, this longing quietly endures, shaping the hidden architecture of our desires. And when, by grace or destiny, we encounter it embodied in another human soul, that person can become our sustenance—an elixir we turn to again and again, yearning for the reunion of something ancient and sacred within ourselves.

Such is the fuel for our Soulmate Addiction.

CHAPTER 4

THE PERIL OF ETERNAL LOVE: THE THREADS OF ADDICTION

In case you foolishly forget, I am never not thinking of you. Virginia Wolf

Lexie closed the door gently as she stepped out into the fading light of day. Inside the building behind her remained the man who had quickly become the epicenter of her inner world, and a ripple of unease passed through her. She, who had always governed her emotions with precision, now found herself unable to steer the course of her feelings for him.

She had always been the architect of her own calm—poised, composed, the master of both her inner and outer landscapes. But everything had shifted the day she met Liam. He was attractive—of that there was no doubt. But beauty alone had never fazed her. In her world of managing a high-end spa, she was surrounded by it daily and was also very much attuned to subtle energy and the vibes of those she encountered. And yet, the moment her gaze locked with Liam's deep brown eyes, something inside her pinged—quiet but unmistakable.

Her friends had long teased her with the nickname "Ice Queen"—not out of coldness, but because she remained untouched by the whirlwind romances they so often chased. With her long brown hair, flawless olive skin, and aqua blue eyes, she certainly was at no loss for attention from men and women alike. Lexie had always longed for that rare, soul-stirring love, but it had so far eluded her. She'd had a few serious relationships—deep, even beautiful in their own ways—but they had either faded with time or burned out in the heat of opposing desires. She had loved, even twice profoundly, and those men would have made wonderful husbands. Still, something essential had always been missing.

She had seen glimpses of this deeper love in a rare handful of couples. It was a knowing. An ineffable pull. A soul-recognition. A timeless current that ran deeper than logic, deeper than desire, yet elusive to many. Stirring, intoxicating, and inspiring to those who recognized it, and puzzling to those who didn't. For most others—even those who seemed genuinely happy—relationships appeared rooted in something more grounded: partnership, mutual respect, and affection. These pairings seemed absent in ways that she could never fully explain, even to her closest soul-sisters who spoke in energy more than words.

Lexie had been brought on six years ago to manage the flourishing spa, and as the business continued to grow, the owner sought ways to elevate their serene corner of the world—transforming it into a sanctuary of complete self-care. That vision soon expanded to include a massage practice, seamlessly folded into the center's offerings. It was through this evolution that Liam entered Lexie's orbit.

He'd only been at the center a few months, setting up his massage studio and carefully curating a team of therapists to bring his vision to life. According to the owner, he was the perfect fit—a transplant from Seattle, starting fresh in the Bay Area to help care for his mom as she dealt with a health issue. He was calm, kind, undeniably attractive… and single. But Lexie knew that wasn't what captivated her. She had met plenty of men who were all those things. This was different. This was something she had never encountered in all her years of self-awareness and careful discernment.

It wasn't just attraction. It was an unnameable ache that stirred beneath the surface of her every moment. When he was near, she felt inexplicably whole, as though some deep alignment had just clicked into place. But when he wasn't—when he left the building, or even when she merely sensed his absence—that wholeness fractured. The longing that surfaced wasn't romantic in the traditional sense. It was energetic. Elemental. A yearning not just for his presence but for something she couldn't quite define. It transcended emotion and bypassed logic. Even a text, a glance at his name, or an image of him online was enough to calm the ache—for a time.

Lexie had never considered herself incomplete. On her own, she had always been "whole" and hadn't needed anyone to validate or define her. Her path had been one of conscious self-work, of knowing and owning her wholeness. Between her spiritual practice and the deeply nourishing connections she cultivated with her closest friends, she was grounded—confident, clear, and vibrant. She was well aware of the pitfalls of looking for anything outside herself to make her feel happy and whole. Until now.

Now, she felt disoriented and unmoored. The carefully cultivated calm that had long defined her was unraveling. She didn't want this ache, didn't welcome this magnetic pull that had upended her balance. It actually infuriated her, even as it compelled her. She yearned for clarity, for answers—anything to explain why her center had shifted so suddenly and so irreversibly. Like a switch had been flicked, a page had been turned, a door had opened to reveal an infinite inner terrain she had never known existed. Lexie did not want to feel this maddening distraction, and it alarmed her at times that she was no longer was the person she had been. Unbeknownst to her, she never would be.

As the opening line of this book suggests, *They say love is a drug—but what happens when your soul provides the ultimate addiction?* At the heart of Lexie's troubles was not simply infatuation or romance—it was the intricate dance between the brain's reward circuitry and a connection that reached far deeper: a Soulmate bond. We are never just our brains. And we are not just our souls. As French philosopher, Pierre Teilhard de Chardin explained: "We are not human beings having a spiritual experience. We are spiritual beings having a human experience."

Most of us have heard these words in various forms, but it is worth noting that although we are more than the visible, we operate through a fragile, ever-demanding physical human vessel. We need clean water, a roof over our heads, nutritious food, and clean air to breathe. And that is just our physical forms. Our brains need positive reinforcement, stimulation, social connection, stress management, and downtime. Our emotional selves need purpose, security, connection, validation, support, and love.

Our human forms are vulnerable in this physical world, but in our true nature as souls, we are boundless—timeless, eternal, indestructible, and magnificent beyond our wildest imaginings. We move through lifetimes carrying the subtle signatures of who we have been: our wounds, our wisdom, our deepest truths. Our souls know no edges, no divisions. They exist in perpetual expansion, in the infinite unfolding of love and creation. So, when a love rooted in that level of existence meets the confines of a human body and mind, it can feel…Suffocating. Conflicted. Like eternity bound in chains.

Layered within this spiritual intensity and the needs of the human form is the exquisite machinery of the brain—a fragile yet brilliant organ capable of flooding our being with a symphony of neurochemicals. These biological messengers—dopamine, oxytocin, and serotonin—conjure some of the most euphoric states we know. Intoxication. Longing. Bliss. Anyone who has ever fallen deeply in love has felt the spell: sleepless nights, unshakable distraction, electric joy, and a sense of magic just beneath the surface of reality.

Behind our enchantment lies a layer of biology, spinning its ancient, alchemical dance. This whirlwind of emotion is nature's way of ensuring humanity's continuity—and while reducing such a profound human experience to mere biology may seem to strip it of its magic, these hormones are both tangible and purposeful, orchestrating an intricate dance that shapes our emotional lives.

Dopamine, the brain's reward messenger, is deeply entwined with both the ecstasy of love and the pull of addiction. When we encounter something pleasurable, this powerful neurotransmitter floods the brain's reward circuitry, evoking a rush of euphoria. In its wake, a chorus of other hormones joins in, orchestrating a sublime symphony of emotion that shapes our inner world and reinforces the behaviors that bring us joy and fulfillment. Dopamine is one of the powerful factors that draws us irresistibly toward a beloved, weaving their presence into our thoughts and dreams. It can bestow upon them an aura of enchantment, casting them as singular and luminous—so extraordinary, it feels as though they alone light up the world around us.

Meanwhile, serotonin, the regulator of mood and attention, lends its signature to love's obsessive edge. It fuels the looping thoughts, the distractions, the yearning that refuses to be quieted. Love's intensity, its bittersweet ache, often echoes serotonin's pull—simultaneously comforting and maddening.

Then there is oxytocin—the "cuddle hormone"—released through physical closeness, tender touch, and deep trust. It envelops us in warmth and fosters a sense of safety and bonding. Uniquely, oxytocin functions within a rare positive feedback loop: the more we connect, the more it flows, reinforcing closeness and encouraging further intimacy.

Topping this irresistible chemical mix are our beloved endorphins. These morphine-like molecules offer calm amid the emotional storm. They ease pain, both physical and emotional, and provide a natural high that comforts us in moments of vulnerability. Paired with dopamine, they create the intoxicating rush familiar to runners and lovers alike—a surge that softens life's sharp edges.

Together, these chemicals do more than serve biological imperatives; they help to compose the symphony of love. They blur the boundary between science and soul, between chemistry and connection, as they weave their magic in the depths of our brains. Within this dance is both the fragility of our human form and the vast, uncontainable brilliance of the spirit, for while our souls recognize the eternal connection, our brain's chemistry sets the stage for biological bonding. Whether we see this chemistry as divine design or a poetic fluke of evolution, the result is the same: a sense of magic, of wonder, of the extraordinary.

What's not to love about falling in love?

However, within all of this heady mixture lies a darker paradox, for several of these hormones can sometimes play a duplicitous role. The very chemicals that help to lift us to dizzying heights can also lead us into the darker waters of craving, fixation, and bondage.

Dopamine, the harbinger of joy, can also be a subtle and insistent taskmaster. With each wave of euphoria, it quietly strengthens the brains neural pathways that bind the thought of our beloved to pleasure—anchoring them in our minds as a source of emotional reward. What may begin as a soul-deep recognition gradually entwines with the circuitry of the brain, transforming the connection from something purely spiritual or emotional into something undeniably neurological. We come to crave their presence not only with the heart and soul, but with the body and mind. A single note of their voice, a memory, a familiar scent—and suddenly, we ache for more.

For some—particularly those predisposed to obsession, compulsion, or addictive tendencies—this dance becomes a powerful vortex. The chemical high lays a track for longing, a pathway that soon bypasses logic and moderation. The desire to connect intensifies, eclipsing reason, as the brain begins to chase the next surge, the next spark. Gradually, and almost invisibly, the bond evolves into an unrelenting hunger—not just for closeness, but for fusion. It is no longer a simple yearning to love, but a deep, consuming ache to merge, to dissolve the space between self and the other entirely.

As addiction progresses, the brain undergoes a metamorphosis, its very architecture shaped by neuroplastic changes. The once-receptive dopamine receptors lose their natural responsiveness, demanding escalating levels of the source of the addiction in order to sustain the pleasure. Simultaneously, the prefrontal cortex, guardian of decision-making and impulse control, succumbs to impairment, further complicating the struggle to break free from the clutches of addiction, even in the face of glaring consequences. When the fixation is a living, breathing person, the complexities can be extreme.

We may make phone calls we should not have, send messages we will eventually regret sending, or show up on doorsteps that we should not be standing on. We might offer our hearts to those unworthy of our trust, spend time or money we cannot spare, betray the ones who depend on us, or even abandon the life we've carefully built—all in devotion to source of our addiction. Under the spell of this neurochemical storm, we may be willing to sacrifice everything because the addiction is calling the shots.

When dopamine levels drop, the addiction doesn't quietly fade—it aches. It claws at us with relentless longing and a desperate craving for relief. Our brains are on fire with the fierce need for one more hit to soothe the pain. A glimpse of an old text, a social media stalking session, the sight of a car like theirs, or the holy grail of being near them again can momentarily lift the anguish. These fleeting encounters offer a temporary balm as the brain releases a trickle of feel-good chemicals. And when we're hurting, we don't just want relief—we want it now. But that momentary comfort comes at a cost—with the craving satisfied, the addiction is reignited, and the cycle begins anew. The pain returns, the hunger sharpens, and the cycle begins again, keeping us in a circular state of misery.

If all of this sounds a little familiar, then we may have entered a state of what many behavioral therapists would call "love addiction" —but that term might not tell the whole story. To some degree, the early stages of love often mirror addiction, and that intensity is natural and even beautiful. Love, in its infancy, is meant to intoxicate. Even so-called "normal" love addiction exists on a wide spectrum, and not everyone who experiences intense emotions in a relationship is necessarily a true love addict.

Yet for those who have crossed a certain threshold into prolonged, consuming emotional states that defy logic or ease, the experience can be deeply painful and disorienting. Trying to explain such love to those who haven't lived it often leads only to blank stares, well-meaning advice, or quiet dismissal. Even within professional circles, modern psychological frameworks frequently overlook one vital possibility: that some of these bonds are not merely psychological patterns or behavioral loops, but reflections of a deeper soul connection—something ancient, undeniable, and not easily unraveled.

So let's get back to Lexie's story.

In Lexie's case, her soul may have recognized Liam—but her brain, with its exquisite sensitivity and susceptibility, had then made him her most beautiful obsession. Lexie had slipped into the first stages of love addiction, but it was no run-of-the-mill behavioral affliction. This was something deeper—what felt like an undeniable pull, as if something greater had woven invisible threads between them, guiding them back into each other's orbit. And from the soul's standpoint, eventual reunification would not be denied.

Like water forcing its way through a tiny break in a dam, the release from the years of waiting, wondering, and silent longing unleashed all of the pent-up power of separation as it flowed in a driving desire for reunification. Lexi's addiction soon took the wheel as she began maneuvering for more connection with Liam.

She shifted her routine to create opportunities for connection. She stayed late at work, hoping to see Liam on his way out. She rescheduled lunches and skipped plans with friends, wanting to be nearby in case he happened to take a break.

Every glance from his eyes, every murmur of his compelling voice, every tiny little engagement with him served to build more and more momentum in the drive for the solace that those connections would bring. Sometimes even just seeing a car similar to the one he drove sent her heart jumping and her soul soaring. Like a cold glass of water on a scorching hot summer day, just a moment of connection with the energy of Liam would satiate her longing for just a little bit as the dopamine poured into her brain, and her soul felt a momentary reprieve from its single-minded driving purpose.

Over time, her thoughts started to loop. What was he thinking? What did he mean by that glance? Why did he say that? Her mind became caught in the same current her heart had already surrendered to. She started to measure her days by the chances she might see him again. Part of her knew this wasn't sustainable. Part of her was quietly alarmed, even embarrassed by how far she was falling. But the pull was too strong. The sweetness of it, the intensity, made it almost impossible to resist.

As she sank deeper into this strange new state, Lexie began to feel isolated. When she tried to talk about what she was going through, her friends brushed it off as a harmless crush. They didn't understand—and how could they? To them, it seemed like temporary infatuation. But Lexie knew this wasn't just a passing feeling. It was something she couldn't name, but it was very real.

Consumed by a whirlwind of emotions and a deep sense of being misunderstood, Lexie withdrew further from her friends, and the world beyond Liam faded. Nothing else felt as alive or as meaningful as being near him. Every other connection in her life seemed insignificant by comparison, leaving her unable to relate meaningfully to anyone who hadn't felt this kind of overwhelming pull. Unfortunately for Lexie, that included everyone she knew.

Even more astonishing were the strange, almost magical experiences Lexie had begun to encounter—fleeting metaphysical moments that left her both unmoored and uplifted. They stirred within her an effervescent joy she hadn't felt since childhood—light, electric, and inexplicably radiant. There was a new brightness in her soul, a buoyancy that seemed to rise from nowhere. It had no clear cause, yet it shimmered with a quiet certainty. For the first time in years, she felt vibrant. Hopeful. Happy. Alive.

As she stepped out of the house that day, her thoughts, as always, were consumed by Liam. Would she see him? Would there be a chance to talk? Perhaps even a few stolen moments alone together? These questions swirled in her mind as she started her car, and just then, a voice on the radio caught her attention: "Come out and see

Liam! He will be waiting for you!" She blinked in surprise before realizing it was merely the tail end of an advertisement for a car dealership. Still, the uncanny coincidence made her smile. A few minutes later, as she pulled into the spa's parking lot, her gaze fell on the bumper sticker of the car in front of her: "Soulmate Sensations." The bold lettering and logo suggested it was the name of a band, but the timing was uncanny. The word Soulmate had just been lingering in her mind as she toyed with the idea of whether such a bond could exist with Liam.

Naturally, she had taken to searching online for answers to her strange and overwhelming experiences, and the stories she found about Soulmate connections had struck a chord. The way people described this rare and transcendent love felt intimately familiar, and for the first time, she didn't feel so alone—or on the brink of losing her mind. Before meeting Liam, she had been skeptical about the concept of Soulmates—dismissing the tales of star-crossed Soulmate lovers as little more than cases of obsession, codependency, or fantasy. But now, everything felt different. With each passing day, she grew more certain that she had been wrong. Soulmates were real, and she was coming to believe that she had found hers

And the synchronicities and experiences kept on coming. Tumbling into her life in never-ending, delightfully unexpected ways, she welcomed every single one. She had always considered herself to be grounded and practical, but through this process, she began to see the world in a completely different way. A more positive way. A more magical way. All of this made Lexi long for someone to talk things over with.

Eventually, she decided to try seeing a counselor, but given the reception she received from her family and friends when she tried to explain her experiences, her expectations were low. Still, she was desperate to find someone who might understand what she was going through and help her navigate this painful journey. The counselor listened attentively as Lexie shared a carefully edited version of her recent experiences. She was hesitant to dive too deeply into all of her recent strange happenings and feelings for fear of being judged, but she should not have worried. The counselor was gentle and kind, as she explained to Lexie with a charming well-meaning intensity all about "obsession", "love addiction", and "hormonal imbalance" with regard to romantic relationships.

Lexie held no ill will toward the counselor as she shut the office door behind her and headed to the car. Sitting in the driver's seat and pausing to reflect, she recalled how the counselor had had no idea what she was talking about when Lexie gently brought up the frequent synchronicities and unexplainable luminosity of her days. Lexie laughed and shook her head as she started up her car and drove away. Clearly, this wasn't the place where she'd find the answers she was searching for.

While it's entirely true that there are many people who fall into love addiction as a result of childhood trauma, low self-esteem, fear of being alone, mental health conditions, or other factors, it's also very true that many of those situations may involve a true Soulmate or Twin Flame. Love Addiction, like other forms of behavioral addictions, can be complex and multifaceted, and seeking therapy or counseling can be beneficial for individuals struggling with this disorder in order to explore the underlying causes, develop healthier coping mechanisms, and build more fulfilling relationships. For many people, however, the start of an addiction to another person began lifetimes or even eons ago, and this compelling and underlying complication is not yet understood, treated, or even acknowledged by conventional medical professionals.

At the highest levels of consciousness, we are all extensions of the Divine—individual waves destined to return to the infinite ocean of Source. In this journey, reuniting with our Soulmate represents a pivotal and sublime step along a seemingly endless path of evolution, as their energy will feel most like our own. From the perspective of the human heart bound to this earthly plane, such reunifications feel like coming home—our one true sanctuary. The mere sight, sound, or energetic presence of these kindred spirits can stir an exquisite ache, awakening a longing so intense that it may border on anguish. When circumstances prevent union, this longing can deepen into a psychological and even physical torment—a reminder of both the beauty and the burden of such ethereal connections.

As Lexie found in her journey, when both the subject of our addiction and the antidote to our pain is our very own Soulmate, the intensity of attachment is heightened, the connection is irreplaceable, and it all adds layers of complexity to the already intense emotional turmoil. The Soulmate element can magnify the emotional stakes, transforming the struggle into something far more challenging than the experience of a conventional "love addiction."

And this, inevitably, made things difficult. As is often true of timeless connections, Lexie and Liam found themselves moving through different stages of their journey. Lexie, attuned to the rare and powerful bond between them, felt the searing pain of their emotional distance. Her heart was open, ready to embrace the strange, beautiful force that seemed to flow between them. Liam, meanwhile, was navigating this intensity from a different shore. Though he sensed something almost otherworldly about his connection with Lexie, the magnetic pull she exerted unsettled him. Distrustful of its origin and wary of surrendering to what felt like a treacherous current, he recoiled. Instead, he turned his attention to safer pursuits—other priorities, distractions, and concerns—seeking refuge from a connection he did not yet understand.

As Lexie slid into a full-blown Soulmate Addiction, it further complicated an already difficult situation. The adage "absence makes the heart grow fonder" rang especially true here, as Lexie's timeless connection with Liam—one she instinctively knew transcended the ordinary—only accelerated her descent into obsession. Soulmate Addiction often takes root in the fertile ground of such eternal connections, but the absence of reunification or reciprocation can cause it to flourish even more. This longing creates the perfect conditions for the brain's dopamine cycle to take hold: fleeting moments of connection, followed by uncertainty, then punctuated by sporadic reconnection, leaving the mind teetering on the razor's edge of exhilaration, pulling Lexie deeper into the addictive loop.

While caught in her obsession, Lexie longed for Liam to awaken to the truth of their connection. Yet the reality of such agonizing situations remains: we cannot do the inner work for someone else—we can only do it for ourselves. We can share our perspective and hold space for them, but we cannot walk their path or hand them answers that are truly theirs to find—let alone answers they may not be ready to receive. Many of these soul-level connections start in ways that feel perfectly natural—intense, obsessive realizations of an otherworldly bond. Over time, such consuming intensity can evolve into enduring, healthy, and wonderfully uncommon partnerships that stand the test of a lifetime. Others conclude after offering each other years of growth and expansion, as one or both individuals have given and learned all they can from the connection in this lifetime. Still others become truly toxic connections, or will never reach the reunion stage at all. It is primarily these last two that cause the deepest, most excruciating Soulmate addictions.

So what is our role in this? It begins with unpacking our own emotional baggage. As individuals, we possess the freedom to shape our own narrative and make our own choices. No matter how deeply we perceive our connection to another, the path we imagine traveling together, or the unexpected turns it may take, the only journey we can truly steer is our own. Our domain begins and ends within the realms of our own heart and soul, and it is here where the healing journey of a Soulmate Addiction resides.

At its core, Soulmate Addiction is a collision of the brain's reward system with the ineffable pull of an eternal connection. While love is often painted as a spiritual force, it is equally shaped by a powerful neurochemical dance—dopamine-fueled euphoria, serotonin's obsessive grip, oxytocin's intoxicating embrace—all conspiring to bind us to the object of our affection. This potent cocktail, while exquisite, can also be perilous, pulling us into cycles of longing, craving, and addiction when the connection remains unfulfilled.

Yet, we are not merely creatures of biology; we are luminous beings navigating a human experience. As Lexie's journey reveals, Soulmate Addiction is not always rooted in trauma or dysfunction—sometimes, it is the soul itself demanding reunification. But when the bond is unbalanced, when one awakens while the other remains unaware, the resulting anguish can be excruciating. It is in these moments that the lesson becomes clear: no matter how fated a connection may feel, our true power lies in our own healing.

Ultimately, love—whether mystical or mundane—is meant to elevate, not imprison. The journey through Soulmate Addiction is not just about finding the Divine within another, but about rediscovering the Divine within ourselves.

Now let's explore the roadmap through this enigmatic addiction.

CHAPTER 5

ETHEREAL ROADMAP: RECOGNIZING AND NAVIGATING UNHEALTHY SOULMATE ATTACHMENTS

If you love deeply, you're going to get hurt badly. But it's still worth it. C.S. Lewis

In every life, there is light and there is dark.

When caught in an unhealthy Soulmate relationship, it may help to remember that there are timeless lessons to be learned that can only be experienced through this unique lens of human existence. These relationships, while rare and often excruciating, carry the potential for profound soul-level growth. To walk this path requires extraordinary strength, resilience, patience, and a deep well of compassion—for both ourselves and the one who has mirrored so much back to us.

With the assistance of many Divine sources, our lessons are planned long before we take our first breath. Our first meeting with a Soulmate often serves as a pivotal stop along a vast spiritual highway. This journey has no map to guide us but plenty of ethereal road signs to steer us along our way. The curious thing about this pathway is that there is no destination. It's through our participation in the stories of love and heartbreak, connection and disconnection, realizations and missed opportunities that we find our greatest transformations along the Soulmate and Twin Flame trail.

Though painful, this journey can serve as a catalyst, expanding our consciousness and inviting us into deeper understanding of who we truly are. Along the way, we are asked to honor the highest calling of our spirit while tending to the complexities of our human life with as much grace and integrity as we can summon.

While this chapter cannot speak to every unique experience, it serves as a guidepost—a starting point on the journey toward recovery and wholeness. It is a reminder that we are not alone in what can feel like an isolating and all-consuming experience. There is hope. There is recovery. And there is a meaningful life beyond the pain.

There is a sacredness in tears. They are not the mark of weakness, but of power.
They speak more eloquently than ten thousand tongues.
They are the messengers of overwhelming grief, of deep contrition, and of unspeakable love. Washington Irving

For the fortunate few, this journey culminates in a lasting, uncommon bond—a relationship marked by deep love, unwavering support, and unparalleled companionship that surpasses ordinary human connections. For many traveling the Soulmate addiction journey, however, there is a much more enigmatic path: It is difficult to fathom that a soul so deeply intertwined with our own could inflict such immense pain, but these relationships often bring unimaginable heartache.

In the initial stages of Soulmate relationships, the sense of home, love, and safety can be so overwhelming that we drop our defenses and expose our deepest vulnerabilities far sooner and more intensely than we might have otherwise. While our spirit recognizes this soul as one we've cherished for eons, the reality of our human experience often includes a legacy of unhealed wounds—childhood traumas, addictions, or other challenges that can manifest as destructive forces within the relationship. These complexities remind us that the journey is as much about growth and healing as it is about love and connection.

Relationships can take countless forms: emotionally abusive, controlling, codependent, one-sided, neglectful, clandestine, toxic, competitive, full of unresolved conflict, defined by trauma bonds, complicated by incompatible attachment styles, narcissist behavior, or serial cheating. The list goes on and on. Profound soul connection does not preclude us from the difficulties of the human condition… in fact, it almost invites it!

The very qualities that make these otherworldly connections so remarkable—deep soul recognition, love, psychic understandings and awakenings, a sense of home and belonging, and the feeling of cosmic alignment—can also lay the groundwork for deep dysfunction and heartbreak, compounding the struggle of a Soulmate Addiction. The sheer intensity of these connections heightens both their beauty and their peril. To soar so high in the pursuit of divine connection is to risk a devastating fall, one that can feel like it is shattering the soul in ways ordinary relationships rarely do. This risk is compounded by the addictive nature of these connections, which can turn heartbreak into a prolonged and deeply wounding trauma. It's not so easy to just walk away from a piece of one's soul, and it's even harder when the drive for union with them has also become a full-blown addiction.

That's not to say that this path is not worth it, even taking into account all of these possible trials, tribulations, and uncertainties. For those fortunate enough to journey through life with their Soulmate, it promises an adventure rich with extraordinary love, connection, soul growth, and unparalleled companionship. And even if the journey ends in a painful descent, we will have soared where few dare to go, living and loving in ways most can only dream of.

The Runner and Chaser Syndrome

Liam wasn't one to invite trouble, nor was he convinced he had room in his life for romance. For years, it had just been he and his mother after his father walked out when he was thirteen. He had eventually carved out an independent life in Seattle, building his career and identity far from home. But when his mother was diagnosed with a rare form of leukemia, there was no hesitation—he dropped everything to return. Liam dedicated himself fully to her, standing by her side through the exhausting ordeal of treatment and recovery. By some stroke of luck, he landed the ideal professional arrangement: a partnership with a thriving business that allowed him the flexibility to prioritize her care. Though life was far from simple, he had found a fragile equilibrium—one he could navigate, at least for now.

What he hadn't counted on, however, was Lexi; She had become an unexpected and consuming focal point in his life. Lexie wasn't vying for his attention, nor did she do anything remarkable to justify his fixation. And yet, Liam found himself drawn to her in a way that defied all reason. When she was near, he felt an inexplicable energy coursing through him, a kind of euphoria he had never known. It wasn't just attraction; it was deeper and more elemental, as though her presence magnified his very existence. She made him feel more alive, more vibrant, and—disconcertingly—more unmoored. The intensity unnerved him. It was as if he were being pulled into her orbit by a force he couldn't see, let alone resist.

The sensation was thrilling but also deeply unsettling. Liam liked control—relied on it. It was how he managed his life, his success, and the chaos of the Universe. But with Lexie, control slipped through his fingers like water. In its place was something raw, uncharted, and electric, both exhilarating and terrifying. He couldn't rationalize it, and the lack of understanding left him uneasy. It felt dangerous, like standing on a frozen river, sensing the power of the current surging just beneath the fragile ice. This strange, consuming intensity left him wary, guarded, and restless in her presence. He realized that Lexie—entrancing, radiant, all five-foot-four of her—terrified him. The realization made him laugh bitterly. How absurd, to feel such fear over someone so beautiful and kind. And yet he knew it wasn't really her that scared him. It was what she had awakened within him and what she represented. The force that pulled him toward her wasn't hers—it was his. A primal, unrelenting power he couldn't ignore, no matter how much he wanted to.

And so, Liam ran.

He distanced himself from her, from the strange and beautiful chaos she stirred within him, leaving Lexie to navigate the uncertain terrain of their connection alone. For Liam, the unknown felt too dangerous, too volatile. He clung to the illusion of safety, refusing to take the plunge into something he couldn't control—even if it meant walking away from something real, something extraordinary.

This "runner and chaser" phenomenon often unfolds as a common pattern in the paths of Soulmates, though it is far from the only one. While Lexie had awakened to the mystical bond that connected them, Liam remained unwilling to take the leap into the depths she had already embraced. Though he saw her as everything he might want in a partner, something deeper within him stirred unease. His intuition hummed with a force he couldn't ignore, urging him to pay attention. For Liam, that inner voice felt less like a beacon and more like a warning. So, instead of seeing it as a call to explore, he took it as a directive to stay far away. And so, he chose distance—leaving Lexie with the agonizing weight of their untold story.

It is not unusual for one partner to awaken to the rare nature of their connection while the other lags behind or, for various reasons, chooses to run. Often—and heartbreakingly—the runner either fails to recognize the depth of this bond or is overwhelmed by the immense and unseen forces it represents.

This fear takes many forms: a loss of control, abandonment, the vulnerability of being fully seen, the possibility of losing oneself within the relationship, or the sheer terror of embracing something so powerful and unfamiliar. Most commonly, they fear failure—rejecting the gift of their dreams feels less devastating than reaching for it, falling short, and losing everything. Partnering with someone where the stakes are lower feels like a safer, more manageable choice. Much of this goes on beneath the surface in the deep subconscious, where our darkest fears and insecurities reside—sometimes, our most precious gems are guarded by our most terrible dragons. Attachment styles, emotional wounds, trauma responses, and countless other factors can contribute to this dynamic, but the outcome remains the same: one partner runs from the otherworldly connection they share and the possibilities of a life few will ever have the opportunity to embrace.

For the chaser, this period can be agonizing. Recognizing the connection does not grant permission to pursue the relationship without regard for boundaries, and respecting the other person's choices *is the only viable path forward.* While this leaves one half of the union stranded in emotional limbo, tormented by the unfulfilled promise of a Soulmate bond, and vulnerable to the pull of Soulmate Addiction, there is life after this heart-wrenching time.

Though each Soulmate story will come to its own unique conclusion, for many Soulmates, the runner and chaser dynamic need not always signify the end of their road. In fact, traces of this energy often persist even within the fabric of deeply fulfilling, long-lasting Soulmate partnerships that started out with one partner as the runner. Though this scenario is a common and major ingredient in the development of most Soulmate Addictions, it is also a common ingredient in the initial stages of many successful relationships! No single factor seals the fate of a relationship, just as no two Soulmate journeys are the same—we cannot look to another's path to illuminate our own.

Impossible Paths

For Jason, Andrea embodied everything he had ever dreamed of for a mate. Beautiful both inside and out and grounded in financial, emotional, and mental stability, she wasn't just the perfect match on paper—she was so much more. Before meeting her, he had never imagined that such profound love could exist, and over time, Jason became absolutely convinced that Andrea was his true Soulmate.

Their connection elevated him to a higher plane of consciousness, enriching every aspect of his life—not just those directly tied to her. Energetically sensitive and aware and no stranger to the mysterious workings of the Universe, Jason had encountered his share of enigmatic experiences. Yet, the synchronicities connected to his bond with Andrea were unlike anything he had ever known. These unusual, unexplainable events seemed to accompany her presence. Whether she was near or simply on his mind, they appeared again and again, forming a thread through his life that felt both mysterious and undeniable.

Jason had long walked the winding road of spiritual growth, confronting and conquering his inner demons in his quest to become whole, grounded, and successful in his life. Yet, every encounter with Andrea shattered his equilibrium. Her presence sent him tumbling from the spiritual ladder he had so carefully climbed. The intensity of his feelings for her—an agonizing mix of longing and impossible love—tormented him. Andrca was everything: radiant, kind, intelligent, funny, and alive with an energy that felt otherworldly.

She was also married.

And so, Jason pressed on, walking his long road alone. Yet amid the solitude, a single stroke of unexpected fortune lingered in his memory: that quiet evening when the two of them had stayed late at work, locked in a quiet struggle with a stubborn technical problem long after the others had gone. Being alone with her in that quiet space felt like a dream. Her presence filled the room with a strange, soothing warmth—a sense of "home" he had never felt with anyone else.

As Andrea leaned over a screen, absorbed in thought, Jason found himself lost in her energy, his soul drinking in the moment. It wasn't until she softly murmured, without lifting her head, "You can breathe now," that he realized he'd been holding his breath. Embarrassed yet unable to contain the surge of emotion rising within him, the words escaped him before he could stop them.

"I love you. I always have. And I'm so sorry for that." Andrea looked up, and in a voice raw with truth, she replied, "I love you too, Jason. I've felt that way since the day we met." The dam broke, and what followed was an evening flooded with emotional release as they spoke of the torturous, winding emotional and spiritual journeys that had led them to this moment. It was a night of shared truths, of souls laid bare, and of love both beautiful and excruciatingly impossible.

At the end of that night, Andrea asked him to never speak of this again. She could not be with him. With three little girls at home and a husband who deeply loved her and was kind, loving, and supportive, leaving for her own selfish gains was unimaginable. He felt she was being a true martyr. And it left him an unwilling one.

Adrift on a life raft built for one and with no end in sight for the longing and pain, so far, his courage to break free and move forward in his life had been no match for his desire to wait for her until the end of time. Little did Jason know that there WAS a path through this—but it would take time, perseverance, commitment, courage, and wading through an immense amount of pain.

He had been waiting, hoping, praying, and yearning for over six years since that day for something to change, without an ounce of anything in the physical world to show him that it would. His friends and family had no idea why he wasn't dating and often tried to set him up with likely matches, but to no avail. Jason felt that he couldn't share his private torment with anyone, and this isolation only served to amplify his agony and loneliness.

For those who have discovered their Soulmate or Twin Flame in this lifetime yet find them achingly out of reach, the journey can be among the most excruciating trials of the heart. Whether separated by promises and commitments, cultural divides, geographical distance, societal constraints, health challenges, substance dependencies, or countless other circumstances, the pain of recognizing this soul connection without the hope of union can lead to a deeply unhealthy and relentless cycle of longing. This path often spirals into chasing, bargaining with oneself, the Soulmate, or the Universe, and an inevitable struggle with addiction—whether to the unattainable person or the dream of a life together that remains beyond reach.

But even the deepest ache, when held long enough, begins to shift. And in time, something within Jason began to quietly stir—a recognition that while love may open us, it is not meant to imprison us. He began to understand that the purpose of this connection was not possession, but transformation. Slowly, painfully, and with no dramatic moment of clarity, he started to gather the scattered pieces of himself, reclaiming his life not in defiance of the love he felt, but because of it.

Jason would never forget Andrea—how could he? She had been the mirror, the fire, the sacred wound. But he was beginning to see that healing did not mean forgetting. It meant honoring the love by choosing to live, to grow, to rise. The path forward was still hazy, the pain still present, but now—finally—he was walking it.

Unhealthy Love

Bryan was everything Lydia had ever dreamed of as a mate. Attractive, intelligent, well-spoken, successful, and seemingly totally, completely enamored with her.

When they had met, she had felt an odd little ping. Like something was off. Or on. It was as if the Universe really wanted her to pay attention to this man standing before her. Lydia usually liked to take things slowly in relationships, but there was nothing slow about how things took off after they met, and it wasn't long before they were spending every spare second together. It wasn't like she *needed* him. It was more like she *was* him—like they breathed for each other and thought each other's thoughts. The resonance between them was so synchronized and the natural gravitational pull so strong between them that there seemed to be no point where Lydia ended and Bryan began. It was an inexplicable bonding that she could not put into words, and no one she knew seemed to be able to relate or understand what she was experiencing.

There were so many days that she honestly could not imagine being any happier. The most intriguing coincidences kept cropping up, particularly when she and Bryan were together. She would be telling him about a brindle dog she once knew, and suddenly, a brindle dog would walk right across their path. She'd be thinking of how great it would be to go get some ice cream, and Bryan would suddenly ask her, "Would you like to get some ice cream?" Even her musings on abstract theories often aligned with the topics of the books he happened to be reading. These moments felt magical—a playful and exhilarating dance between their minds and the Universe.

However, as their relationship progressed, Lydia began to uncover a darker undercurrent in their story.

Increasingly, she found herself swept into Bryan's world of avoidable crises—chaotic episodes that deeply disrupted her life and eroded her well-being. These storms, often rooted in his emotional volatility, lapses in judgment, or reckless decisions, dragged her into a whirlwind of angst and upheaval and left her bearing the weight of losses and compromises she hadn't chosen. Still, the turbulence would eventually subside, the familiar magic would return, and Lydia reassured herself that Bryan was simply navigating his way back to stability after challenging years.

But the cycles of chaos proved unrelenting, returning with cruel regularity when she least expected them. Adding to her anguish was a pattern Lydia found even harder to reconcile: Bryan's unsettling habit of delivering sudden, cutting remarks. Though he often lavished her with affection, praise, and attention—what she would later recognize as "love bombing"—his barbed comments struck with icy precision. They often came unprovoked, leaving her stunned and questioning whether she had imagined them. By the time she fully grasped the pain, the moment had passed, and she found herself uncertain how to address it. The interplay of enchantment and wounding left Lydia in a precarious balance, caught between the intoxicating highs of their connection and the bewildering lows of its shadows.

When she began to broach the subject of these difficulties with him, choosing her words with care and calm, the "Bryan Bomb" would detonate. Instead of hearing her out, he would deflect and retaliate, launching attacks on her supposed shortcomings as a partner, parent, or person. The original issue would vanish beneath a storm of accusations, guilt, and misdirection. This pattern left her disoriented and emotionally drained. Bryan's arguments were often cloaked in clever manipulation and tangled in nonsensical "word salad," making it nearly impossible to resolve the heart of the conflict. Over time, these cycles of chaos and manipulation began to erode Lydia's happiness and self-assurance. The effects seeped into every corner of her life in ways that defied easy explanation. Night after night, she went to bed with a knot of tension deep in her stomach and awoke with a slight feeling of dread and anxiety. It was tarnishing nearly every aspect of her life—her work and finances, relationships with friends and family, even how she felt about herself.

By then, Lydia was living with Bryan—a decision she came to regret, recognizing it as the outcome of his relentless love bombing and subtle coercion. Yet, each morning as she met his gaze, the inexplicable, magnetic bond between them would stir once more. In his eyes, she glimpsed not only the man she had fallen in love with but also the fragile, wounded boy he kept hidden beneath the surface. Her heart would soften, the soul connection would flicker back to life, and for a fleeting time, the darkness seemed to lift. But the reprieve was always temporary. The cycle inevitably resumed—a relentless rhythm of light and shadow that kept her ensnared in a love as transcendental as it was perilous.

What Lydia could not yet see was that she had walked into a devastating blend of two powerful forces: the intoxicating pull of a Soulmate connection and the addictive grip of a relationship with a narcissist. While classic narcissists can weave insidious traps, the stakes are even higher when intertwined with the synchronicities, soul-level resonance, and overwhelming love that often defines a true soul connection. This convergence created a path not only riddled with pain and entrapment but also one that demanded immense growth—a crucible for some of Lydia's most difficult and transformative life lessons.

Substance Abuse and Addiction

Ethereal and soft-spoken, Veronica was the voice that greeted Matthew when he called back to the office. Her quiet confidence and effortless ability to resolve his rare dilemmas had a way of brightening his day. There was something otherworldly in their connection, and it wasn't long before they found themselves in a relationship. From there, things moved quickly. He'd never felt such a strong bond with anyone, and for the first time, Matthew found himself entertaining the possibility that there might be some truth to all of those Soulmate tales he had once dismissed.

As their relationship deepened and their life together began to take shape, Matthew started noticing subtle inconsistencies in her stories and actions—small gaps that tugged at the edges of his peace of mind. Feeling an uncomfortable disquiet, he began to pry and observe until he eventually found the cause. Veronica had arrived in his life with a deeply hidden secret—an addiction so strong and deep that nothing could shake her out of that driving need for a fix, and it slowly and inexorably began to replace every connection that they'd ever had. Determined to save his Soulmate, Matthew threw himself into the fight. He staged interventions, sought out rehab programs, pleaded, bargained, and even wielded the sharp edges of tough love. But nothing worked. Yet, abandoning his Veronica seemed unthinkable. It was hard to see life beyond his love his Soulmate, and part of him did not want one.

His friends and family, watching from the sidelines, saw what Matthew could not: his unwavering devotion was destroying him. Gaunt, exhausted, financially drained, he was sinking under the weight of Veronica's demons. In trying to save her, he was losing himself. Veronica was his addiction, and being addicted to an addict had consumed everything he had ever worked for or built. There was no in-between. There was life with Veronica, and there was no life. His friends and family did not understand that, and yet—just as he continued trying with Veronica—they continued trying with him.

One day, fate intervened in a twisted tale of good fortune. Matthew found himself lying on the living room floor, staring blankly at the ceiling, unsure of how he had ended up there. His body, once resilient through years of turmoil, had finally reached its breaking point. As he pulled himself upright, the truth struck with undeniable clarity: the stress of Veronica's addiction—and the relentless battle to save her—was killing him. His body, his last dependable ally, had sent a message he could no longer ignore.

For Matthew, it took years of destruction and a critical health crisis to confront his addiction to his Soulmate. While Soulmates can offer an unparalleled depth of connection and love, they can also present us with choices that feel nearly impossible to navigate. Addiction to an addict is an area of Soulmate love that can be difficult to travel alone, and seeking help is advisable for those suffering through this journey. Programs like Al-Anon and Nar-Anon, designed for the families and friends of addicts, provide a compassionate framework through their 12-step approach. Therapy, hotlines, and other support groups can also serve as invaluable resources on this arduous journey. Though the Soulmate connection itself may remain unaddressed, the universal truths of loving someone struggling with addiction are deeply understood and supported within these spaces.

Of course, addiction is not the only challenge that may surface within our Soulmate relationships. These ethereal connections can draw out a spectrum of deeply rooted struggles—mental health issues, abuse, neglect, infidelity, codependency, personality disorders, and more—all emerging as unexpected teachers on our path. Within the intensity of eternal love and Soulmate Addiction, such trials often carry the seeds of our greatest lessons.

Navigating the Unhealthy Soulmate Connection

Should we find ourselves entangled in an unhealthy Soulmate connection, it may offer some solace to remember that we belong to a rare circle of souls that is presented with such a profound level of growth and transformation. The path through such a bond calls for immense strength, unwavering faith, deep resilience, patience, and compassion—not only for our Soulmate, but for ourselves. And yet, within the turbulence lies the possibility of awakening to extraordinary depths of self-awareness and expanded consciousness. Along the way, we are asked to walk the highest path of our spirit, while still honoring the realities of the physical world with as much grace and intention as we can offer.

This chapter is not meant to capture every variation of an unhealthy Soulmate experience, but rather to serve as a guidepost—a starting point on the journey toward healing, clarity, and wholeness. It is a reminder that we are not alone in what can feel like an isolating and all-consuming experience. There is hope. There is recovery. And there is a meaningful life beyond the pain.

This section has been focused on recognizing those Soulmate and Twin Flame relationships that are unhealthy, toxic, and damaging. What has not been addressed in this chapter is truly abusive relationships. If one is suffering abuse in a relationship, it's important to consider the options for walking away. While this book touches on the soul aspects that may be present in such a situation, it does not address the danger and necessity of immediate escape. Professional assistance may be called for, as leaving can be both complex and fraught with risk. Abuse is never justified—end of story.

For unhealthy Soulmate Addiction dynamics that do not involve abuse, the initial steps toward recovery involve more reflective action and are the most pivotal in our journey. These early strides unlock the door from the relentless cycle of dysfunction and suffering, guiding us toward a path of healing and recovery. The choice to take these steps is deeply personal and cannot be made for us. But when we are ready to move forward, beyond the anguish of Soulmate Addiction lies the promise of a life that can contain much love, light, and happiness.

One of the first steps involves understanding what a Soulmate is to us and what they are not. While the soul is eternal and can ultimately never be harmed, unhealthy Soulmate relationships can feel like a slow erosion of self as the pieces of our identity are gradually chipped away with each compromise we make, lie we tell ourselves, or twist in our Soulmate road—until we are left with questioning who we really are. The pull of this rare connection can be so overpowering and the addiction to them so irresistible that even in the face of devastating or destructive pain, we remain drawn to the spirit that lies beneath our partners' toxicity.

While the term "trauma bonding" has traditionally been used to describe the bond that can develop between a victim of abuse and their abuser, it is also frequently used to describe the common attachment that develops when two people who have suffered past trauma connect through their shared pain. While it is not uncommon for shared trauma bonds to masquerade as a Soulmate bond, it is also very common for them to exist *in* a Soulmate bond. The broken pieces are what draw us in, and the soul bond is what delivers us to our suffering journey together. This type of bonding is one of the common forms of emotional glue that tie Soulmates together in the face of unhealthy attachment, but it is certainly not the only possibility. The complexities of our potentials can be beyond understanding in our human form—from trauma bonding to personality tendencies to past life influences, a large and largely unseen ingredient mix can go into baking the cake of our Soulmate Addiction. What we often lose sight of, however, is the cost we are paying for buying into what we believe is our soul's story.

Being Soulmates does not mean the Universe mandates that we must spend our lives together—especially if one or both of us are toxic. It may serve as a reason—or more accurately, an excuse—we tell ourselves to remain in a harmful or destructive relationship. The path is a complex and often treacherous one to navigate. While at our core, we are all magnificent souls, radiating beauty and power beyond imagination, how many of us truly step into that limitless potential?

It's important to see our Soulmates as they are in this lifetime, not as the potential we see reflected in their eyes nor through the echoes of what they may have been in the past. Our Soulmates are not embodying the beings they once were in another lifetime or even a few decades ago; they are living the reality of who they are now. And that might not be meeting their intended potential in this lifetime. The question is, "What are we going to do with it?"

As the boundaries, borders, cracks, and crevasses emerge between two Soulmates, we often cling to the belief that this person is a literal piece of our soul and so convince ourselves —if that is the case—that the pain and challenges must be surmountable. This narrative feels comforting, because it aligns so neatly with the story we long to see unfold. "When my Soulmate finally steps up and learns their lessons, stops running, or addresses their deep flaws, we will finally create the beautiful life we are meant to share!" After all, if this is a true Soulmate connection, surely there must be a divine plan for unification? Why else would the Universe bring two deeply bonded souls together only to place insurmountable obstacles in their path?

And yet, the truth is often more complex and less romantic. For most of us, this life is meant to be one of not only joy, happiness, and great love, but also a journey of growth and learning. The Universe does not always promise resolution in this lifetime, but it does promise to provide us with the circumstances and support to live our greatest experiences and become our greatest selves. Indeed, many of our significant relationships—including those rooted in soul connections—were preplanned. These bonds, no matter how challenging, are meant to shape us—not always to fulfill the idealized story we imagined. For some, that means a long and happy life with our Soulmate, yet for others, it is a life of expansion through the path of our pain.

While it may offer little comfort, the Universe is fully aware of the challenges we are facing. For many, this idea may be infuriating—how can we reconcile the unbearable pain, isolation, and loss of hope with the notion that everything remains part of a divine order? Adding to the weight of this realization is the possibility that we, at some soul level, may have had a hand in shaping this journey with our Soulmate—such a thought can feel almost too much to bear.

So, while this difficult time can feel like a mistake or wrong turn as we find ourselves feeling angry, confused, and lost in the "what ifs" and "why me's" of the pain, nothing goes to waste on our soul's journey; every experience contributes to our evolution. Navigating this unpredictable, twisting river may be one of life's greatest challenges, but it can also become one of its greatest gifts. As most of us have experienced, heard from friends, or read in other people's life stories, sometimes a situation that holds unbearable pain leads us to a place that we could never have reached on our own. And often, the nature of the human experience means that the full shape of the journey becomes clear only when we arrive on that distant, uncharted shore.

As we travel this path with so many unseen pitfalls and challenges, one of our greatest fears is that this Soulmate journey is our one true shot at a love of this magnitude in our lifetime. And perhaps the hardest fact to bear is that it that it may be. That, above all else, is the belief that keeps us hooked into the pain. Therapists can tell us otherwise and books and stories can paint a rosier glow of other "fish in the sea", but the reality remains: this person may indeed be a soul match unlike any other we are destined to encounter.

Yet, equally significant truths exist—truths that, once accepted into our very core, hold the power to transform our journey from one of anguish and despair to one of hope, possibility, and eventual happiness. They stand as counterbalances to the gripping belief that we will never find another like our Soulmate, or feel this way again.

One of these truths is that we *truly can never know what is in store for us.* The visions we conjure of a life without our Soulmate—days, months, and years steeped in emptiness—may feel like an unbearable void, but this "all-or-nothing thinking" is a cognitive distortion. A thinking mistake. A mental trap that magnifies and prolongs our pain.

The real truth is, we don't know if our Soulmate love is our greatest relationship possible in this lifetime, or if our souls are destined to eventually intertwine again sometime in the future. Nor do we know whether or not another equally extraordinary connection awaits us.

Despite countless romantic stories and theories of Soulmate and Twin Flame partnerships, the mysteries of the soul remain just that—mysteries. Do souls sometimes split into more than two? Are there multiple soul matches for each of us? What purpose does this connection serve on our journey? What lessons did we come here to learn? How long will our journeys last? Though there are many opinions, the true answers elude us, so it is wise to resist the urge to bear the weight of a lifetime of imagined loss. If we must go there, it's imperative that *we do not stay for long*. Our ego mind may want to control the narrative and steer our journey, but the fact of the matter is—when it comes to the journey of our soul—it has no control at all. We must engage with the present moment and allow greater forces to guide our sails without an ability to see ahead past the horizon.

It's also worth considering that—even if we had ended up with our Soulmate—the reality of that relationship might have brought us even more pain than we feel now. As hard as the current struggle is, a life with our Soulmate could have destroyed us. The longing in a Soulmate connection can be so overwhelming that it blinds us to the deeper truths: perhaps our personalities would clash in ways that erode happiness over time, or maybe our Soulmate hides additional or deeper wounds—narcissism, infidelity, addiction, or countless other unseen burdens. Sometimes, the ingredients we're given in this earthly version of a Soulmate bond simply aren't enough to create the lasting, divine feast we dreamed of.

The Indian mystic and yogi Sadguru once said "And so these are the only two things that you are suffering right now: your memory and your imagination." Many Soulmate Addictions occur before we really wade into life's relentless challenges with our love. The idealized version of our Soulmate love and partnership often eclipses the mundane truths of daily existence—the car payments, the wailing toddlers, the Sunday night blues that arrive in anticipation of Monday. Over time, the trials and mundane nature of life can test even the most profound Soulmate connections—slowly transforming initial infatuations into a slow, heart-wrenching decay, or forward into soul-filling growth and connection.

Falling in love with an idea—the vision of a perfect life or an idealized partner—can become one of our most painful illusions, as real life can never truly compete with our projections and fantasies. The greatest Soulmate relationships are not the ones that arrive fully formed, forever frozen in a state of bliss, but the ones that can be nurtured and maintained through life's ordinary, imperfect moments. So much of what we often mourn in times of agonizing longing is not the loss of a true, tangible reality but the loss of a dream—a future that exists only in the mirage of our minds. And sometimes, the Universe protects us from our greatest desires.

So, though our pain may push us to the brink of what we thought we could bear and we may not be able to see light on the horizon, it is still there—waiting for the tiniest shift in our perspective, lift in our vision, or release of the blinders we have been holding onto for so long. It is only then —when a chink appears in the armor of our beliefs—that we may find another way through the agony of Soulmate Addiction.

Now let's step into the fire of heartbreak as we take our first steps toward healing.

CHAPTER 6

THE HEARTACHE OF HEARTBREAK: COPING WITH SOULMATE DISILLUSIONMENT

The heart will break, but the broken live on. Lord Byron

Katie's eyes brimmed with tears as she entered my office, emotion tracing quiet paths down her cheeks. She settled into the chair with a weary grace, her words spilling out in halting fragments—pieces of a love story that had once felt like fate but had unraveled into something unrecognizable.

It had all begun in the most unassuming way: a work meeting held online. The moment she heard Jamal's voice, something inside her shifted. She had always been a pragmatic woman, grounded in logic and routine, yet his voice carried an inexplicable echo of familiarity, a sense of home. She felt an immediate, magnetic pull that she could neither explain nor cared to resist. When fate placed them together in a breakout session, that subtle spark deepened into something undeniable. The connection was immediate and quietly powerful.

Katie fell hard. And fast. Never before had she experienced emotions of such depth and breathtaking intensity. She had always dismissed notions of Soulmate love, yet suddenly, she found herself engulfed in it. She was consumed by the magnitude of her emotions, unable to think of anything but him. It wasn't like her to be swept away so completely, and at times, she feared she was losing herself. Their bond was uncanny, and conversations felt effortless—as if they shared a single mind. They uncovered peculiar, impossible coincidences between them, a fascinating web of experiences and understandings that defied reason. She had loved before, but nothing like this. Gradually, her world oriented itself around him. Each thought, each choice, each passing moment seemed drawn into his orbit, until the rest of her life faded quietly to the edges. In his presence, everything else receded.

Before Jamal, she had considered herself whole. She hadn't known she was missing something—something she had never even imagined existed. Now, she felt expansive, more herself than ever before. The phrase "finding your other half" had always seemed like a poetic illusion, yet suddenly, it felt achingly real. She pored over articles on Soulmates and Twin Flames, trying to make sense of what she felt. Her anxious attachment style—so often a source of tension and restlessness in past relationships—was quieted, soothed in ways she hadn't thought possible. Love had always been a delicate dance of uncertainty, but with Jamal, she had finally found solid ground. For the first time, she felt safe in love and at peace, as though she had arrived exactly where she was always meant to be.

Until he began to pull away.

At first, she couldn't make sense of it. It felt inconceivable—like watching something sacred unravel before her very eyes. She stood helplessly by as the world they had so carefully built began to fracture, Jamal growing more distant, unreachable, a shadow of the man who had once felt like home. He refused to speak of it, unwilling or perhaps unable to articulate what was going on. When she finally pried the truth from him, his words were fragmented and uncertain, but the meaning was clear: the intensity of their love was suffocating him.

His past held the key. Jamal had been raised by a mother who had lost herself in the pursuit of a love she would never receive—desperate for the attention of an abusive husband, and eroded by rejection until she turned to alcohol to numb the pain. As a child, he had watched her diminish and observed as her addiction and neediness dissolved her into something weak, helpless, and discarded. He had sworn never to become that vulnerable, never to need someone that much. To him, love was a trap—a dangerous abyss from which escape was impossible. His childhood wounds had shaped him into a man who equated closeness with entrapment, desire with suffocation. To love with such depth, to need with such intensity, felt like an unbearable surrender—an annihilation of self. Jamal had arrived at their Soulmate reunion carrying the weight of an avoidant attachment style, shaped by childhood wounds of low self-worth and conditional love—wounds that had long taught him that closeness was a risk too great to take.

So, while Katie reveled in having never known such love, never having felt more at home in another's presence, that same love—so intoxicating to her—had become unbearable for him. What she experienced as sacred unity, he felt as quiet suffocation. The intimacy that soothed her anxious heart stirred unease in his—tightening around him like an invisible noose, and sending him spiraling into panic. For her, their love was healing; for him, it reopened wounds too deep to bear. She had overlooked the subtle signs of his discomfort, too enraptured by the beauty of what they were building to see its cracks forming beneath. Until, at last, the world she had believed to be unshakable collapsed around her. Her perfect world. In the end, it was not a lack of love that drove him away, but the weight of fear—his past pressing in, childhood ghosts resurfacing, and the unbearable vulnerability of needing someone too deeply. And so, he did the only thing that had ever made him feel safe. He ran.

Katie could do nothing but watch as the love of her life—the man who was her Soulmate—became a stranger, walking away from everything they had built. He left, and with him, he took the future she had dreamed of.

Sometimes, love is not enough. Even Soulmate love.

As C.S. Lewis once wrote, n*o one ever told me that grief felt so like fear.* And indeed, it can be terrifying. We are left to face the darkest corners of our psyche—the fear of abandonment, the fear of emptiness, the fear that we've lost something eternal. When it comes to an unhealthy Soulmate or Twin Flame Addiction, fear and grief are inescapable. While all relationships bring pain in their own way, this path—so often marked by emotional volatility and spiritual intensity—carries with it a unique kind of devastation. When the connection shatters, it can feel as though the very fabric of our being has been torn apart. Our heart still beats, but it feels broken beyond repair. A dull ache coils in the pit of our stomach; dread greets us with the morning light. The agony of aloneness presses heavily on our chest, and—like fractured ribs encasing a wounded heart—our pain remains invisible to others, though every breath is laced with suffering.

The memory of "home"—of that magnetic, otherworldly bond—echoes in our soul, while our mind spirals through once-cherished moments: shared laughter, whispered promises, and the incredible psychic connection that seemed written in a language only our souls could understand. Sleep becomes elusive as our mind replays the what-ifs and maybes, and thoughts torment us in the quiet hours of the night, waking us in the morning with the hard brick of knowledge that our Soulmate or Twin Flame will not be walking with us on our path of life. Grief surges in waves more powerful than anything we've ever known. Without them, the future stretches before us like an endless road paved with solitude and pain.

The loss of our Soulmate is not just an experience—it is an all-encompassing upheaval of body, mind, and soul. Each thought, each longing, each memory becomes both a trigger and a dagger, piercing through our emotional armor and deepening wounds we never imagined possible. This pain is not confined to the heart alone; it reverberates through the body in ways both profound and undeniable. Grief can unleash cascades of stress hormones, igniting inflammation, joint pain, digestive distress, cardiac strain, headaches, exhaustion, and restless, haunted nights. Social withdrawal, depression, and anxiety can follow as we are left with the unbearable task of continuing forward in the physical world while feeling the anguish of losing or walking away from what feels like a part of our very own soul.

In our desperation, many of us seek refuge in anger—anger at our beloved, at the Universe, at ourselves. The grief of losing an ordinary love is agonizing, but the severing of a Soulmate or Twin Flame connection can be excruciating beyond measure. The life we thought we would be living is over. It may feel much like death—our body still moves, and our mind responds to the outer world, but we are a walking, emotionless, and hopeless shell that can see no future. This grief does not simply stem from missing another person—it is the unbearable absence of a part of ourselves.

For those who have experienced this depth of connection, a Soulmate is not merely someone we love—they are an extension of our very being, a shared consciousness inhabiting two separate forms. When that bond is broken, an unbearable isolation can take its place. Loneliness becomes a constant companion, for once we have merged with another, how can we settle for only being half? Who are we without them? What shape does life take beyond their absence? To the outside world, everything appears unchanged—our reflection in the mirror remains, our voice echoes as it always has, our routines carry on: work, home, familiar faces. And yet, within us, everything is forever changed. We are irrevocably altered. Like an invisible ocean devouring the contours of a once-stable shore, the grief surges in waves, dissolving the inner architecture we thought was permanent. It erodes our sense of identity, washes away old certainties, blurs the boundaries of self—and pulls us into uncharted depths. Depths we never asked to enter, yet must now learn to navigate.

For many, this grief shifts the focus from the external—the pursuit of careers, possessions, and social status—to the internal, drawing us toward the vast, uncharted terrain within. As we walk through the fire of loss, what once held value may begin to feel hollow. A career once pursued for prestige may now seem like an empty vessel. The social gatherings and circles that once brought a sense of belonging may no longer nourish the soul in the way they once did. This transformation reshapes not only our inner landscape, but also our place in the outer world. Relationships may begin to strain, not from lack of love, but from misalignment. Friends and family may struggle to understand this quieter, more contemplative version of ourselves—the one now marked by wisdom gained through grief and by a hunger for the sacred that no longer finds nourishment in the mundane.

In the stillness of this wreckage, our attention turns to the unseen—to the sacred, the mysterious, the eternal. We begin to crave what cannot be bought or measured: truth, connection, presence. And though this rebirth may alienate us from the familiar, it also opens the door to a deeper alignment—with ourselves, with the Divine, and with a life no longer shaped by surface, but by soul.

One of our greatest challenges can be the unspoken expectation that others will understand this pain. But just as an old soul is shaped through many layers of experience, others too are evolving through the lessons of their own journey. Their path may not yet have led them to this depth of feeling, leaving them unable to fully meet us where we are. Well-meaning but uninformed advice, offered in an attempt to comfort, can instead widen the distance—leaving us feeling even more separate, misunderstood, and alone. In response, we may feel compelled to hide our pain and wear a mask of normalcy, pretending to be unchanged when, in truth, we are forever altered.

At the same time, while this suffering is deeply personal, it can become even more isolating to feel that no one else could possibly understand it. Reaching beyond the belief that our journey is ours alone can help—whether through a book like this one, a YouTube channel that speaks to our experience, or by connecting with someone who has traveled a similar path. If we can begin to recognize it as a thread in the vast tapestry of human experience—woven through with the grief of many others—we begin to find a quiet doorway back to connection. Seeking solace among those who have walked this path can be a balm to the soul. They, too, carry the marks of sorrow and the understanding it leaves behind, and in them, we may glimpse reflections of the depth we now hold.

Throughout all this, we come to find that grief is not our enemy. It is a temporary friend that brings us catharsis, flow, and the power of renewal. Complete healing from the loss of our Soulmate relationship means forging through long lengths of pain—surviving a journey of a million invisible steps through blazing infernos of grief that seem to stretch without end. Yet if we surrender to this grief and allow ourselves to feel the pain, granting it access to the deep recesses of our hearts, its flow through the center of our being can soften the sharp edges of brokenness, bringing light where once there was only shadow.

Still, healing demands a delicate balance. We must allow grief to flow through our body, mind, and soul, yet temper its weight with the gentleness of self-preservation. To drown in sorrow is not the goal; rather, we must grant ourselves only as much mourning as we can bear in each moment. The descent into despair is part of the process, but it must be tempered with quiet acts of self-care—petting the cat, stepping outside for a walk in nature, tending to life's small, steady rhythms. In honoring both our sorrow and our survival, we carve a path forward, one step at a time.

It's through…grieving that acceptance arrives. Sheryl Paul, *The Wisdom of Anxiety*

In our heartbreak, as we detach from an unhealthy Soulmate relationship, a moment arrives when the pain and grief of hanging on to any shred of hope outweighs the agony of letting go. When we reach this point, the chains that have bound us to our long suffering begin to loosen, creating space for the Universe to intervene and guide us toward healing. As Einstein famously said, "Nothing happens until something moves." Once we set our intention toward a new path, the possibility of a different future emerges. Though this stage can be excruciatingly painful, it also holds the promise of deep evolution in ways we cannot imagine from where we stand at the beginning of our journey

In her seminal work *On Death and Dying*, Elisabeth Kübler-Ross introduced the five stages of grief: denial, anger, bargaining, depression, and acceptance. While this model has helped shape our understanding of grief, it is now widely recognized that these stages are not linear steps, but emotional landscapes we may revisit time and again. Healing is not a straight line, but a winding stream that curves and bends, flowing backward as often as forward. It is also not a race, and recognizing our readiness —or lack thereof—is an important act of self-compassion.

While there is no one "right" way to grieve, a healthy process involves allowing our pain to be felt, expressed, and released, rather than trapped within the body and mind. When left to stagnate, unprocessed grief can lodge itself in the psyche, manifesting in emotional, physical, or spiritual distress. Moving grief through the body, whether through tears, writing, speaking, or simply sitting in stillness and listening to where it lives within us, allows the energy to be alchemized rather than buried. Without real processing, acceptance, and subsequent healing, the dark tendrils of Soulmate Addiction can remain dormant, only to resurface later, once again reaching for us with its familiar, destructive allure.

The instinct to escape pain—whether through denial, distraction, or numbing our emotions—can keep us locked in the very cycle we seek to break. One of the most challenging aspects of healing from Soulmate Addiction is the dual grief: the loss of both our Soulmate and of the addiction itself. We grieve not only the physical ending of our bond with them in this lifetime, but also the emotional passion and spiritual longing they awakened within us.

Even if the connection was toxic, it may have stirred parts of our soul that felt more alive, more profound, or more purposeful than anything before. We lose a source of intensity that once gave shape to our days and meaning to our suffering. The addiction filled a void, gave us something to ache for, to chase, to believe in. Without it, we can feel disoriented—like life has gone flat, colorless, and stripped of the emotional highs that once made us feel real—

even when they were laced with pain. In their absence, we are left with a strange hollowness—like a song half-finished or a conversation forever paused. This makes Soulmate Addiction uniquely difficult—it is not merely a heartbreak, but a rupture in our sense of meaning, self, and soul.

As human beings, we are especially adept at spiritual bypassing—sidestepping the depths of our emotions in favor of comforting philosophies, and avoiding the discomfort of true healing by prematurely detaching from grief. We may declare forgiveness while still harboring unspoken rage, or speak of surrender while resisting pain in our bodies. These premature conclusions may feel enlightened, but if not grounded in genuine emotional processing, they are little more than illusions—thin veils that prevent the heart from truly healing.

True transformation asks more of us. It asks that we feel the burn, walk through the sorrow, and meet ourselves in the rawness of truth. Spirituality is not a shortcut around pain—it is the strength to sit with it, to befriend it, and allow it to become a portal to greater depth and light. Our faith, our beliefs, our sacred perspectives—they can be our greatest sources of courage and joy. But even these can become walls if they keep us from the full experience of grief. To heal, we must bring presence to our pain, not just insight. Only then can this evolution take root—not as an escape from suffering, but as the natural flowering of having truly met it. To escape grief, we have to go through it, not around it.

In *The Untethered Soul,* Michael Singer writes that we alone hold the power to give ourselves inner freedom—or to deny it. That truth becomes especially resonant in the wake of Soulmate Addiction. The story of our inner life has been so deeply shaped by this bond—its gravitational pull writing our narrative for us. But now, the pen must return to our own hands. To move forward, we must do what feels most impossible: relinquish even the faintest ember of hope for reunification.

Until we do, we remain stuck—afraid to step beyond, fearing that by letting go, we are abandoning a chance—however slim—that our dreams might still come true. Yet it is precisely these lingering thoughts that perpetuate our suffering. As long as a tiny spark of hope remains, we cannot move forward. Like an alcoholic keeping a single bottle hidden away, we may secretly cling to the possibility of returning to our addiction, fearing that someday we will find that we left it too soon. That glimmer of hope becomes the tether that holds us back, keeping us tied to the agony of "what ifs."

Haruki Murakami once said, *Pain is inevitable. Suffering is optional.* We suffer when we resist change and grip tightly to an illusion that no longer serves our growth. Finding acceptance of the truths of our journey means that we will need to honor the current that brings people both to us and away. If we were hungry, and the most exquisite, nourishing meal was somehow sitting at the bottom of a pot of boiling water, would we reach in and endure unbearable pain to grasp it, or would we resign ourselves to starving? Both paths lead to suffering, but only one offers an opportunity to step away, to experience healing, and have the hope of sustenance elsewhere. It is time to ask ourselves: Is the agony of holding on worth the cost, or is it time to release our grip and reclaim our freedom?

As Tara Brach wrote: *Radical acceptance is the willingness to experience ourselves and our lives as it is.* For those walking the path of Soulmate Addiction, acceptance is the gateway through which all genuine healing must pass. But acceptance doesn't shout. It rarely arrives with fanfare or finality. More often, it slips in quietly—like a soft murmur from the soul, tired of the endless battle and yearning for peace. Sometimes, it rises from the stark realization that the road paved with chaos and heartbreak has finally run its course. Yet it doesn't always mean fully making sense of what the Soulmate experience once was. It isn't a single moment of arrival, but rather a slow unfolding—an evolving truth that reveals itself over time. It may take months, years, or even a lifetime to fully understand it, and that's okay.

Letting go doesn't mean the love wasn't real. It means your soul is ready for peace.
Brianna Wiest

In this journey from grief to acceptance, it can be liberating and wise to take our Soulmate off the pedestal we've placed them on. It's only natural to see them as "more" because, on a soul level, they really are. The connection is real, ethereal, transcendent. Yet what we are addicted to is a living, breathing, fallible human being—a flesh-and-bone person carrying wounds, contradictions, and patterns shaped by their own genetics, gender, upbringing, karma, culture, health, astrological tendencies, education, and countless unseen forces.

In this light, the Soulmate we believed them to be may not reflect who they actually are in this lifetime. Though the soul bond exists beyond time and space, the realities of this incarnation together may not align. This is the paradox we face—the divine essence we see, and the lived reality we must acknowledge. Sometimes, the soul we are bonded to inhabits a person who simply cannot walk this earthly path alongside us. And so we must ask ourselves, with courage and honesty: What exactly are we holding on to?

True acceptance is not passive. It is not giving up. It is the radical act of turning away from the tug-of-war between reality and the illusion of what might have been. It is the quiet, brave decision to make peace with our agonizing loss and let go of the story we so desperately wanted to write—to see clearly what is, rather than what we hoped it could be. We are not defined by loss, or by the dreams that did not come to pass. We are not broken. We are whole. And what feels like loss is often just the shedding of illusion—of who we thought we were, of what we believed the situation to be. Loss, then, is no longer a theft of our wholeness, but a clearing. A letting go. A sacred return.

As we meet this moment with honesty and a willingness to understand, clarity begins to emerge. With it comes the ability to choose—wisely, gently, and from within. Acceptance nurtures resilience. It softens resistance. It reminds us that we are not lost; we are evolving. Eckhart Tolle speaks of making the present moment our ally—of aligning with it rather than opposing it. When we stop pushing against what is and instead move with it, we invite transformation. Struggle becomes strength. Uncertainty becomes wisdom.

We don't need all the answers. We may have none. What matters is that we recognize where we are, honor our experience, and choose to turn inward—toward our own healing. This is the first, most essential step. It is both an ending and a beginning: the threshold of a deeper journey into ourselves and toward our becoming.

When we finally surrender to the truth of our Soulmate experience—and take gentle responsibility for our role within it, clarity begins to emerge. In that light, we start to see the choices that lie before us, the tools that wait patiently at our feet, and the support systems ready to guide us as we take our first, tentative steps toward healing.

Though the path of recovery is deeply personal, it is not one we must walk alone. If anxiety or depression feels overwhelming, seeking help is not a weakness but a sacred act of self-respect. Whether through a support group, spiritual mentor, trusted friend, family, or therapist, external support offers strength, perspective, and the reassurance that we do not have to bear our struggles in solitude. True strength is not measured by how much pain we can endure alone, but by our willingness to seek the light that leads us forward.

Someday —when we have journeyed far beyond this terrible place—we will carry its lessons deep within us, woven into the very fabric of who we have become. Time, both cruel and kind, moves us ever forward—further from the life we once envisioned, and further from the presence of our Soulmate. We may resist its passage, fearing the growing distance, yet time itself is part of the cure. Each morning, we wake to the weight of our loss, settling upon us anew.

We learn to move through the light of day, to endure the quiet ache that drapes itself over us with the setting sun, only to wake again and repeat the cycle.

You are presented with exactly the same sort of country you thought you had left miles behind, says C.S. Lewis. Such is the inescapable nature of grief—it returns to us again and again, often grasping our hearts in the most unexpected and inopportune times on our slow path to healing.

Then, one day, we raise our faces to the warmth of the sun and realize that we have made it. The burning edges of sorrow have softened. Though a quiet ember of grief may remain, nestled beneath layers of healing, it no longer consumes. It glows gently now, not as a wound, but as a reminder of how far we've come. And much like the Japanese art of Kintsugi in which broken vases are repaired with gold, our hearts, once fractured, do not return to their original form. The beauty is in the repair, as we have been rebuilt from within with a light that is even more beautiful, resilient, wise, and infinitely more powerful than we could have ever imagined embodying.

Through our pain, we will rise—not merely restored, but reborn. We have looked into the depths of our own agony and did not drown. Our ballast will no longer shift in the storms of suffering, as we have faced the depths of hell in our own hearts and survived. As we move forward through our lives, we will eventually reach a place where life begins to unfurl again. Color slowly creeps back into our world. Vibrancy once again stirs in the most unexpected places. Life begins to feel full. Yet in unbidden moments of reflection, that ember of grief may flicker back to life, glowing with a familiar ache—a poignant reminder that our soul connection, though distant, will always remain quietly alive.

In the chapter ahead, we'll explore the tools that can support our healing and help to guide us beyond the grip of Soulmate Addiction. Stepping into this next part of our journey requires a quiet willingness to consider a new narrative—one rooted in healing, light, and the gentle unfolding of hope. Though it may have been like no other, our Soulmate love story served its purpose in our past. Now, we stand at the threshold of something new. This is our sacred space in the Universe, and we alone hold the pen—crafting the story of our future that is yet to be written.

Now let's get started on our healing journey.

CHAPTER 7

BREAKING THE PATTERNS: TOOLS FOR BREAKING THE GRIP OF SOULMATE ADDICTION

The deeper sorrow carves into your being the more joy you can contain. Khalil Gibran

Jordan's soul felt on fire as she sped down the highway skirting the Cascade Mountains. With every passing mile, the weight of the past seemed to loosen its grip, slipping away like the last rays of sunlight sinking behind the jagged peaks. The life she was leaving behind in Diablo grew smaller, more distant, and more unreal with every mile put between her and the disaster of a relationship back in that small house between the mountains. Diablo was a good name for the town that had housed her heartbreak. In Spanish, it meant "Devil" —an all-too-fitting description of the man who had shattered her world.

Jordan had thought she'd found the love of her life. And in many ways, she had. She didn't need anyone pointing out to her that their relationship contained incredible ingredients that she had not known could even exist in a relationship. When times had been good, there had been absolutely nothing like it—an electric harmony that made the world shimmer with an ethereal light. When she was in his presence, her soul sang, and she felt truly at home in the Universe in a way she had never felt before. Jordan and Michael moved through life as if sharing one mind, one heart, one soul—their love was synchronicity embodied, a celestial alignment that filled their days with wonder. This life and love were all she had ever dreamt about, and Jordan thought that she would be spending the rest of her days in that place by the mountains with her one true love.

What she could never have foreseen was the silent passenger Michael had picked up along his journey—a hitchhiker lurking in the shadows, unseen in the early years. Jordan could have no way of knowing the destruction this quiet companion would visit upon their worlds, and how it would ultimately destroy hers.

At first, it was just a feeling, a whisper of something amiss. Michael was still Michael, but he seemed restless—as if he were searching for something just out of reach. Subtle shifts became undeniable changes. Over time, this behavior slid into something a little more insidious and malicious, and Jordan became alarmed. The warmth in his eyes cooled, his presence dimmed, and unease crept into their once-effortless harmony. Michael was jumpy, secretive, distracted, and soon letting things slide in his life that he never would have before. He became unkind, untrustworthy, dark in his thoughts, and mean-spirited with his words. Her beloved Soulmate was still her Soulmate, but something dark had wrapped itself around him, slowly consuming the man she used to know.

She tried to hold on. She told herself love could weather anything. But love, no matter how deep, cannot conquer what has already been surrendered. Jordan was devastated. She could never have imagined anything that would force her to abandon the love of her life, but here it was….the unthinkable monster of substance addiction had taken control of her love, and she was powerless to do anything but watch him sink. The Michael she had known—the man who had once been her safe harbor—disappeared beneath a tide of darkness, replaced by a stranger. A liar. A thief. A man who lost his job, his car, his relationships—until all they had built together crumbled into dust. Jordan was left standing in the wreckage, realizing that love alone could not save him. And if she didn't leave, it would destroy her, too.

As the realization dawned that she could not save his life but she could still save her own, she packed her car, dried her tears, and drove away. What she didn't know—but was soon to learn—was that leaving a Soulmate behind is only the beginning. The first, necessary step in the journey from surviving to thriving beyond many Soulmate Addictions.

Eventually, as Jordan settled into a new home and began the first steps to building her new life, she realized that she had carried along her own little hitchhiker—a relentless ache that tethered her heart to the man she had left behind. Her thoughts revolved around him, imagining his pain, his longing, his life without her. In the quiet of the night, her soul still reached for his, the bond between them refusing to sever despite the destruction it had wrought. As the pain and suffering of dealing with his addictions began to fade, her soul cried loudly for its mate in the dark hours of the night. Try as she might, her strong mind could not corral the longing in her heart, and her waking hours began to be completely focused on thoughts of her lost Soulmate love. She was beginning to learn the hardest truth of all: leaving an addiction behind does not mean it leaves you. Walking away from Michael was like an alcoholic setting down a half-finished bottle of wine—the craving, the connection, the desperate longing remained.

The Soulmate Addiction recovery story has just begun.

Exploring Recovery

For the fortunate few, a Soulmate connection gradually settles into a deep and enduring love. With time, the fiery intensity transforms into something profound yet steady, a rare and precious bond that no longer requires survival tools. If we are among those who have reached this place, we can step fully into the love story so many long to tell, and much in this chapter may not apply to that beautiful journey. However, we may wish to read on, as the tools that follow may one day come to serve a friend, a loved one, or even a future version of ourselves.

While "Soulmate Addiction" is not yet a term formally recognized by the medical community—largely because science has yet to acknowledge the existence of the soul—it is a very real struggle, bearing striking similarities to other forms of addiction. And as with any addiction, recovery from Soulmate Addiction is possible, but it demands commitment, the right tools, and the willingness to walk through grief, not around it.

However, while society offers well-established support systems for substance and behavioral addictions—12-step programs, rehabilitation centers, therapy—those navigating Soulmate Addiction often do so in isolation, without a clear name for their pain or a community that understands it. Tools for healing do exist, and many are the same: self-inquiry, support, structure, spiritual practice. Yet what makes this recovery uniquely difficult is not just the intensity of the bond being mourned, but the lack of understanding and empathy surrounding it. Until now, many have been left to navigate their grief in silence, carrying their pain as a private, lifelong burden. However, as awareness grows, so too will the resources available, fostering deeper compassion and recognition of the soul's role in our love stories.

For now, the tools available are varied—some rooted in psychology, others in spirituality, and still others in practical daily discipline. Each person must find what resonates most, leaning into the methods that bring relief while setting aside those that do not. Some tools may prove invaluable at one stage of recovery but lose effectiveness over time; others, once dismissed, may later become sources of strength. The key is consistency—showing up for ourself every day, using the tools that serve us in the moment, and allowing the process to unfold at its own pace.

While we cannot explore every possible recovery method in these pages, we will focus on those most effective for beginning our journey—approaches that offer the greatest impact for the time and energy invested. If any of these tools spark curiosity but are not covered in depth here, we can seek further exploration on our own.

As a society, we have made great strides in understanding addiction, though no true "cure" exists—only the ongoing path of recovery. The same holds true for Soulmate Addiction. What follows are the tools and strategies that will help us regain control, reclaim our sense of self, and begin the process of healing. Though the reality may be painful—accepting that our Soulmate may not walk the rest of this lifetime with us—it is possible to move forward. Beyond the devastation, beyond the loss, a new kind of love and happiness awaits. Our journey does not end here. It is only just beginning.

Tools for Recovery:

No Contact Rule

In the midst of an active Soulmate Addiction, the thought of never again having our Soulmate in our lives can be an absolutely unbearable possibility. The pain can be one of the greatest emotional agonies we ever endure, but when a Soulmate Addiction becomes destructive, toxic, or deeply harmful, the first step toward saving ourselves is accepting, in both mind and soul, the possibility of moving forward without them. Reaching this level of acceptance may take months or even years, but once we can embrace the realization that our Soulmate has become a toxic drug that is poison to our soul, we have reached a foundational step in our healing.

Breaking free from this addiction is no different from quitting any other substance. We cannot heal while continuing to indulge in what harms us. Just as an addict must remove their drug of choice to begin the journey toward wellness, so too must we release our Soulmate in order to reclaim ourselves.

The act of going "cold turkey"—severing contact completely—is not an option; it is a necessity. We cannot move forward until we acknowledge the power this bond holds over us and make a wholehearted commitment to abstain. The No Contact Rule becomes our anchor in the storm, the first and most essential act of reclaiming our lives from the grip of this emotional entanglement. The road to healing begins the moment we resolve to break all ties, without exception.

This process, however, is excruciating. In the early stages, the withdrawal can feel all-consuming, driving an almost irresistible urge to seek contact—through a call, a text, a glance at their social media, or even a seemingly innocent drive past a familiar place. But like any addiction, the first and greatest challenge is resisting the impulse to soothe our pain with another dose of what we crave. Just as an addict must abstain completely to reclaim their life, so too must we sever all ties with our Soulmate if we are to break free from the cycle of longing, suffering, and self-destruction.

True healing lies beyond this stage, and to reach it, we must walk through the fire of letting go. Not because we no longer love—but because we are choosing to love ourselves enough to be free. This is the sacred work of healing: a conscious, deliberate unbinding of the soul, one brave step at a time. With this step, we must reject every form of connection—no matter how small or intangible. This means deleting messages, erasing pictures, discarding gifts, and removing the music, letters, or keepsakes that tether us emotionally to the past. It is a conscious, deliberate act of release—an essential step toward freeing not just our lives, but our hearts, minds, and souls.

The No Contact Rule is the foundation upon which our recovery rests. No amount of self-work or healing practices can be effective if we continue to indulge in the very thing we seek to escape. As long as we allow that energy to remain in our lives—even in shadow—we remain ensnared. The journey toward wholeness begins with one unwavering decision: to remove the very thing that binds us, so we may finally step into the light of our own becoming.

Of course, there are situations—such as co-parenting, shared responsibilities, or professional ties—where complete removal is not an option. These circumstances bring great challenges, but healing is still possible. In such cases, firm emotional boundaries and intentional detachment become crucial, and additional considerations will be offered for this challenging situation as we move through this chapter.

The Letter to Ourself

The next tool is a beautiful gift that we give to ourselves. It is a letter written by us for our eyes only, and it will be one of the most important tools in our arsenal. Once written, it should be kept somewhere safe, accessible only to us. It will become one of the most powerful instruments in our healing, a sacred lifeline when clarity wavers. If used to its greatest potential, it may eventually become dog-eared, soft with our anguished grip, and stained with the tears of our pain and healing.

We cannot think our way out of a Soulmate Addiction. Emotions and cravings cannot be conquered by mere mental analysis. Everything is energy, and in this addiction, our thoughts form an endless loop—cycling through the same obsessive patterns, pausing momentarily, only to spin again without resolution. There are few who truly understand this torment, and even fewer resources to guide us through it.

Without a way to disrupt this relentless cycle, we risk remaining trapped—held hostage by our own mind. Clarity is fleeting, slipping through our fingers just as we grasp it. One moment, we may convince ourselves that our Soulmate is our only true love in this lifetime, that relationships require sacrifice, that the pain is worth it. In the next, a flash of rationality reveals the toxicity, the destruction, the inevitability of heartbreak. We oscillate between devotion and disillusionment, standing in a thousand shifting perspectives, unable to anchor ourselves in truth.

It's not uncommon to place our Soulmate upon a pedestal, shrouding the connection in mysticism and romantic idealism. We tell ourselves, "We are from the same planet", "The Universe brought us together to finally get it right in this lifetime", or "Our love was written in the stars." These beliefs, though poetic and deeply felt, can blur the line between spiritual truth and emotional illusion. And yet—even if our bond is etched in the stars—our choices here on Earth can still lead us straight to the dark side of the moon.

The ethereal nature of a Soulmate connection can tempt us to believe that it lives above the laws of reality, untouched by the ordinary rules of human life. But it does not. A Soulmate who is drowning in addiction will still pull us under. A Soulmate consumed by narcissism will still fracture our spirit. No amount of cosmic destiny can shield us from the consequences of another's unresolved wounds.

It can feel like the cruelest twist of fate—to find our Soulmate, only to realize that being with them is impossible. To find the mirror of our soul in another, and yet be forced to walk away for the sake of our own survival. But the truth is, even Soulmate love must bow to the realities of boundaries and emotional safety. A sacred connection does not excuse harm. And a destined bond does not guarantee a shared path. Sometimes, the lesson written in the stars is not how to stay—but how to let go with grace, wisdom, and gratitude.

And so, in these impossible Soulmate situations, we must turn to our tools. Among them, the letter will be one of the most powerful tools in our arsenal. When doubt creeps in, when longing overwhelms, when nostalgia distorts reality—we will need to be reminded, unequivocally, why this relationship cannot be. Emotions are masterful illusionists, whispering deceitful promises in the quiet hours of the night. But this letter will be our voice of truth.

So let's grab a hot tea, cold drink, or anything that brings comfort as we find a quiet niche to unpack our thoughts and experiences. We can name this letter anything we choose: "Letter to myself," "My Soulmate Addiction Survival Letter," or simply "What I Must Remember." This letter is best written objectively and without clinging to a shred of hope.

This is not the place for "If they change, then maybe…" or "If they seek help, things could be different…" Instead, we must write: "They have not chosen to change. Even if they did, it would take years of growth before they could meet me where I am." All we have is *now*. Now, and the wisdom of experience. The path we have walked with them has led us to this moment—and it is this moment, not imagined futures, that must guide us forward.

This letter is for the version of ourselves who will waver, who will ache for their voice, who will crave their presence in moments of weakness. We must capture, in undeniable detail, the truths that must not be forgotten. The lies they told. The destruction their addiction has caused. The betrayals, the selfishness, the broken promises. The moments that revealed their immaturity, their unreliability, their inability to conquer their demons.

This letter must be a lighthouse in our storm, cutting through sentimentality with the piercing light of reality. Keep it factual. Keep it sharp. Avoid opinion, for opinion can be debated—but cold, hard facts cannot. It's important to write in such a way that reminds our wavering, wobbling, crying-in-the-middle-of-the-night future self of the destructive, toxic aspects of this relationship—a future self who, lost in longing, may try to rationalize, to bargain, to rewrite history through rose-colored lenses.

We will not always feel this clarity. That is why this letter must hold the truth so firmly that even our future self cannot deny it.

Letter to Our Soulmate

The next letter is for our beloved—the one in which we spill our hearts onto the page, unfiltered and raw. Here, we can express our love, scream out our pain, and mourn our shattered dreams. We can even offer understanding, perhaps even forgiveness.

But we must not send it.

This is the hardest part. The longing to share these words with the person we love most will feel unbearable. But it is no longer their business that we love them. It is ours. Nothing will be gained by pressing these truths into their hands—at best, it will end in disappointment; at worst, it will resurrect false hope and needlessly prolong the cycle of pain.

This letter is not for them. *It is for us.*

In ways unseen, our Soulmate will still receive the energy of these words, but they do not need to read them. By anchoring our deepest thoughts and emotions into physical form, we release them from the prison of our minds. We give them to the Universe, allowing it to dissolve the weight of our sorrow—not just for us, but for them as well.

For months, maybe even years, we have been spinning these conversations in our heads. But unspoken thoughts remain trapped within, swirling endlessly in an unbroken loop and resisting the power of the Universe to lend its magic to our healing. This letter—and the one to ourselves—helps to break the spell of circling addictive obsession. It signals to the Universe that we trust it with our pain. And our Soulmate need not lay eyes on the words, as, at a certain level, they already have.

There may be times when writing multiple letters feels necessary, as new layers of grief surface or old wounds demand release. This is part of the process. But no matter how many letters we write, they must never be sent. The time for speaking our hearts to them has passed. That chapter ended with the relationship itself, and it does not need an epilogue.

If we find ourselves agonizing over the need for them to hear us, to acknowledge our pain, to be sorry—know that this is the voice of Ego. The desire to be heard, validated, and understood—these are human needs, but they are also snares. If we are not careful, we may find ourselves with one foot hovering over an emotional mine buried just beneath the sands of our awareness. True healing requires a measure of self-awareness and the ability to recognize when our own inner gremlins are leading us toward danger.

As we step into acceptance and begin breaking free from the grip of this addiction, we must remember: *this journey is about us.* It is about our healing. Setting aside our need for acknowledgment, accountability, or even closure from them is an important part of the process. Their chance to grow alongside us, to benefit from our love, light, and presence, was in the past. Now, our focus must shift—fully, finally—to ourselves and our own healing.

Other Forms of Writing and Journaling

Beyond letters of release and closure, there are many powerful journaling practices that can aid in healing, clarity, and personal growth. These tools, when used consistently, can help untangle emotions, unlock creativity, and guide us toward a greater sense of peace.

One of the most well-known methods is the practice of "Morning Pages," introduced by Julia Cameron in her acclaimed book *The Artist's Way*. This stream-of-consciousness writing—sometimes called "dumping" or "offloading"—is a way to clear the mind, allowing thoughts to flow freely onto the page without judgment or analysis. This practice is meant for our eyes only; whatever arises, we write. Ideally, committing to several pages daily yields the greatest benefits—helping to quiet mental noise, dispel negativity, and free up creative energy. Over time, this ritual can become a powerful tool for breaking through emotional and mental stagnation.

Another deeply impactful practice is "Gratitude Journaling". This can be used alongside Morning Pages or reserved for moments when we need to shift our perspective toward the light. The practice is simple yet deeply transformative: each day, we write down things we are grateful for, no matter how small. The taste of a morning cup of coffee, the comfort of a soft blanket, a kind word from a colleague, or the laughter of a friend—these everyday blessings often go unnoticed, yet they serve as anchors of stability and joy. By intentionally recording them, we train ourselves to recognize the abundance that already exists in our lives.

For those navigating the pain of Soulmate Addiction, "Trigger Journaling" can also be an invaluable tool. In the early stages of healing, countless moments in daily life—an old song, a familiar scent, a shared restaurant—can stir grief, longing, or heartache. Instead of being consumed by these emotions, we can document them. Writing down the date, time, place, and the thoughts or reactions that arose allows us to identify patterns, acknowledge our pain, and explore ways to respond differently. Sometimes, healing begins simply in the act of recognition—understanding that a song playing in a café has the power to unearth memories, but that we, in turn, have the power to change the song, leave the space, or shift our focus. Over time, this practice helps us regain control over our emotional triggers rather than allowing them to control us.

Though all of these journaling methods can be incredibly beneficial, it is important to choose the ones that resonate most. Too many options can feel overwhelming, especially in the midst of emotional recovery. It's recommended that we experiment, explore, and find the type of journaling that supports us best. Some may become lifelong rituals, while others may serve their purpose and fade with time. The key is to remain open, and let journaling be a possible tool of self-discovery, place of solace, and a quiet witness to our journey forward.

Radical Acceptance

"Radical Acceptance" is a powerful concept rooted in dialectical behavior therapy (DBT) and mindfulness practices. At its core, it is the practice of fully embracing reality as it is—without judgment, resistance, or the desperate wish for it to be different. It calls us to acknowledge the present moment in its entirety, including our emotions, thoughts, and circumstances, without trying to change, control, or rewrite them.

Pain is inevitable, but suffering arises when we resist reality—when we fight against what is. In the context of Soulmate Addiction, Radical Acceptance allows us to release this struggle and find peace within ourselves. It is not about surrendering to unhappiness or remaining in harmful situations (and certainly not about staying in abuse), but about recognizing the truth of our experience and choosing to respond in a way that aligns with our well-being.

Thoughts such as *If only I hadn't said that, This isn't fair, or If only I could have helped them overcome their addiction* keep us shackled to the past, replaying a reality that no longer exists. But if we are standing on the other side of that mountain—ready to step into healing—it is time to accept what has been, to see our present circumstances with clarity, and to reclaim our power.

Radical Acceptance reshapes not only our relationship with the past but also with ourselves and others. As we learn to release our grip on things we cannot change, we experience profound shifts—we find that we can let go of the need to control others and develop more compassion for those who are not perfect (including ourselves). We can find peace in the midst of unpredictable life changes, reduce stress as we stop waging war on reality, accept challenges as they arise, and no longer feel overwhelmed as we navigate the present moment.

Once we embrace Radical Acceptance, the foundation for deeper healing is set. From this place of clarity, many other tools and practices can take root, guiding us forward on the journey to true freedom.

Urge Surfing and Coping with Cravings

One of the difficulties of a Soulmate Addiction is that we often feel that we are no longer in control of our hearts and minds. The thoughts, the longings, the excruciating emptiness fills our soul and touches our every waking moment. When our hearts feel on fire with agony, it can be very difficult to not do something we shouldn't to alleviate the pain—such as pull out old pictures of our Soulmate, contact one of their friends to "check in', or even try to contact them ourselves. Urge surfing is a very effective mindfulness technique that is used in substance addiction recovery, but can be equally effective when we need to overcome our overwhelming and destructive urges or cravings in our Soulmate Addiction.

Much like surfing the waves of the ocean, urge surfing involves riding the wave of an urge without acting on it. When an urge arises, instead of immediately giving in or trying to suppress it, urge surfing encourages us to observe the sensation without judgment. Focus on the physical and emotional components of the urge, noting how it feels in the body and mind. Like the waves of the ocean, urges have a natural ebb and flow—gradually rising in intensity, peaking, and then subsiding. Some waves are big, some are small, but none of them last forever. When we imagine our urges as a wave, then with mindful awareness we can acknowledge the urge without engaging with it. By staying present in the moment and allowing the urge to pass, we can learn to tolerate the discomfort for a short time, because we know that once it is gone, we will have made an incredible step in regaining control over our own actions.

As we practice this over time, our urges and cravings will gradually decrease and start to fade, and the practice becomes easier. The ultimate goal of urge surfing is to eventually reduce the waves in our emotional ocean to a barely perceptible rise, and—with the help of other practices—there will come a day when our emotional responses will reflect back only the clear blue sky of freedom from our Soulmate addiction.

Reward and Distraction

There is no getting around the fact that healing from a Soulmate Addiction can be hard work. Amidst the journaling, urge surfing, and conscious efforts to do what is best for us, there comes a time when the inner child within us simply needs a reprieve. A moment of rest. A well-deserved reward.

Maybe it's that special coffee that we rarely allow ourselves to buy, an episode of our favorite show, a long walk, a hot shower, or having some soul-filling food. This road is a marathon, not a sprint, so giving ourselves a break or reward is an important part of maintaining our motivation.

Equally important to our well-being is distraction—a conscious and intentional shifting of focus away from pain and longing. A simple phone call to a friend, a deep breathing exercise when intrusive thoughts creep in, tackling a project we've been meaning to complete, or heading to the gym—these moments of redirection serve as lifelines when the weight of our emotions feels unbearable. Creating a "Distraction List" can be a powerful way to ensure that when we need an anchor, it is already within reach.

That said, it's crucial to recognize the difference between healthy distraction and numbing behaviors. The intensity of withdrawal from Soulmate Addiction can be overwhelming, tempting us to seek relief through alcohol, substances, or other self-destructive coping mechanisms. The pain may feel unbearable at times, but the key to true healing lies in facing it and using our tools to gently move through the process, not anesthetizing it with harmful, inappropriate, or unhealthy habits.

In most normal romantic relationships, there is an element of intensity and distraction, but with an addiction to our Soulmate, it becomes so much more. It's unavoidable that, at least for a time, our Soulmate becomes our obsession. Shifting our focus from our Soulmate to an obsession that is beneficial and uplifting is a powerful way of moving forward in our lives. Painting, writing, cooking, meditation, volunteering, spiritual practices, exercising, or sports are just a few areas in which we can ignite our creativity to bring us more joy and fulfillment.

These new passions may not immediately erase the pain, but they will begin to fill the space that longing once occupied, gently shifting us from a downward spiral of loss to an upward trajectory of renewal. And the Universe? It responds in kind. When we take even the smallest steps toward joy, growth, and fulfillment, we open the door for more of the same to flow into our lives.

Positive Affirmations

The words we say matter. They shape our perceptions, influence our emotions, and ultimately define our reality. When healing from a Soulmate Addiction, positive affirmations serve as a powerful tool, helping to shift our self-perception and the way we engage with the world.

"I release what was, and I trust in what is meant for me," "I am worthy of love that nourishes, respects, and supports my growth," or "This heartbreak is a sacred teacher. I trust the wisdom it brings" are a few examples of affirmations that can become part of our healing toolbox. This process is deeply connected to neuroplasticity—the brain's remarkable ability to rewire itself by forming new neural pathways. Research shows that affirmations can reduce stress responses and activate the brain regions associated with positive emotional regulation. Through the intentional use of language, we can reshape our inner narrative and cultivate a healing mindset for our journey beyond Soulmate Addiction.

Self Love

Whether recovering from a Soulmate Addiction or simply seeking personal growth, embarking on the path of deep self-discovery is one of the most rewarding paths we can take. While we may already be aware of our likes, dislikes, values, and conscious beliefs, true self-knowing extends far beyond these surface-level understandings. It delves into the uncharted depths of our subconscious—the unseen forces quietly shaping our perceptions, choices, and experiences.

Much like the intricate mechanisms beneath the hood of a finely tuned car, the inner workings of our psyche operate largely unseen, yet they are the driving force behind our journey. Things such as our genetic makeup, childhood experiences, cultural conditioning, societal norms, and unconscious hopes and fears all converge to create the unique tapestry of who we are. This complexity makes each of us an extraordinary and irreplaceable facet of existence, while also ensuring that the journey of self-discovery is a lifelong adventure.

When we choose to embrace the exploration and discovery of our inner landscape with an attitude of openness, wonder, appreciation, and delight, we can break the bonds of unhealthy beliefs, emotional patterns, and reactive behaviors. Getting to know this deep part of ourselves brings to our lives empowerment versus victimhood, growth versus stagnation, and the ability to utilize calm consideration versus reactivity.

Our false but deeply rooted beliefs often speak in whispers so faint we barely notice them, yet they can still derail our best-laid plans, hopes, and dreams. Thoughts such as, "This relationship is the best I'll ever have," "They love me, so I must be special," or "Only this person can see my flaws and love me anyway" may seem harmless or even comforting, but they often stem from a subconscious rejection of our own inherent worth and power. When left unexamined, these deep-seated narratives can lead us to settle for less, cling to unhealthy attachments, or misinterpret love as validation rather than a shared experience of growth and connection.

Another key aspect of self-awareness is the ability to differentiate between fear and intuition. Many of us recognize the mystical wisdom that intuition can offer, leading us toward alignment, ease, and unforeseen opportunities. However, without a clear understanding of our inner landscape, what we perceive as intuition can sometimes be nothing more than fear disguised as insight. That sinking feeling in our gut—the one telling us something is off—may not always be a true warning; it might instead stem from a past wound, a conditioned belief, or a deeply ingrained habit of self-protection. Fear is skilled at masquerading as intuition, whispering caution when what we actually need is courage. Growth is often intimidating, and when we stand at the threshold of positive radical change, the subconscious mind may do everything in its power to pull us back into the safety of the familiar.

The best way to navigate through this fog clouding our perceptions is to illuminate our path with self-awareness—by recognizing the outdated fears that no longer serve us while honing our ability to trust the voice of true intuition. This process is not immediate, nor is it always clear-cut, but with time and practice, we can sharpen our discernment and walk with greater confidence toward what is genuinely meant for us. Most of the tools discussed in this chapter serve as pathways toward deeper self-understanding, and countless others are available for exploration. With curiosity and patience, we can continue peeling back the layers of our inner world, uncovering those deepest truths that have always been waiting for us beneath the surface.

Social Support

Without someone to talk to who understands our pain and the intensity of the journey, it can be a very lonely road. Unlike ordinary heartbreak, this experience carries a weight and emotional range that few can comprehend. Well-meaning friends and family often offer familiar yet hollow advice—"You'll find someone new," "You need to move on," or "Just get over it." Though spoken with good intentions, these words fail to meet the depth of our suffering, leaving us feeling even more isolated, unheard, and disconnected.

Over time, many Soulmate Addiction sufferers retreat inward, finding it too painful to explain an experience that others simply cannot grasp. At the same time, time alone is not always our friend on the path of Soulmate Addiction recovery. While solitude can sometimes offer space for reflection, too much time alone can deepen our sense of despair. Finding a person, a community, or a group that understands this journey not only provides emotional validation and support, but reminds us that we are not alone, we are not broken or irrational, and we *do* have a future of love and connection ahead of us.

Group Therapy and Support Groups

Twelve-step programs such as Co-Dependents Anonymous (CoDA), Sex and Love Addicts Anonymous (SLAA), Love Addicts Anonymous (LAA), and Adult Children of Dysfunctional Families (ACDF) offer invaluable community and structure for those on the path to healing. These group-based programs provide a safe and supportive environment in which individuals can work through the 12 steps of recovery alongside others who share similar struggles.

While there is currently no official 12-step program dedicated specifically to Soulmate Addiction, these groups may still serve as meaningful spaces for growth, insight, and emotional support. For those navigating this unique and often isolating experience, an emerging healing community is being cultivated*. To stay informed on future offerings and available resources, please visit SoulmateAddiction.com.

Emotional Freedom Technique

Emotional Freedom Technique, or EFT, is a scientifically supported self-help method that gracefully merges the wisdom of ancient Chinese acupressure with the insights of modern psychology. Often referred to simply as "tapping," EFT involves gently tapping on specific meridian points on the body while consciously focusing on an emotional or psychological concern. These meridian points are channels through which energy flows in the body, and tapping on them releases blockages and restores balance to the energy system.

Backed by over a hundred studies attesting to its remarkable efficacy, EFT has been used successfully to address a wide spectrum of issues, including anxiety, addiction, depression, trauma, phobias, and chronic stress. Whether practiced independently or with the guidance of a skilled therapist, EFT is valued for its simplicity, accessibility, and empowering effect.

A typical EFT session begins by identifying a specific emotional challenge. Once named, its intensity is assessed on a scale from 1 to 10. Then, a setup phrase is created—something like, "Even though I'm not with the love of my life, I deeply and completely accept myself." With this phrase in mind, the tapping sequence begins. (A quick online search or the companion Soulmate Addiction Workbook will provide a guide to the recommended meridian points.) After completing the sequence, the intensity of the emotion is reassessed. Often, it will have noticeably decreased. This process can be repeated as needed until emotional relief is achieved.

EFT offers a deeply effective pathway for dissolving the gripping emotions—such as anxiety, longing, and heartache—that often accompany the experience of Soulmate addiction. It is a gentle yet powerful tool for emotional healing, helping us regain a sense of control over our emotions, peace, and inner alignment.

Mindfulness

Mindfulness is the experience of being fully present, aware, and conscious of the present moment. Wayne Dyer once said that "Peace is the process of retraining your mind to process life as it is, rather than how we think it should be." In Soulmate Addiction recovery, mindfulness plays a huge role in recognizing the stories we tell ourselves and illuminating the hidden fault lines in our minds.

Research has shown that mindfulness not only alleviates suffering in addiction recovery but is also among the most effective tools for healing the addiction itself. By embracing mindfulness, we learn to let each moment be exactly as it is—rather than how we wish it to be.

A simple yet powerful entry into mindfulness is focusing on the breath. Deep, intentional breathing anchors us in the present, allowing us to observe our thoughts with non-judgmental awareness and extend gentle compassion toward ourselves. The average person has as many as 60,000 thoughts per day, and in the throes of Soulmate Addiction, these thoughts can be relentless—triggering memories, fears, and longings. Mindfulness grants us the ability to witness these thoughts without becoming entangled in them, replacing destructive patterns with those grounded in truth.

As discussed in other practices here, journaling can be an invaluable tool in a mindfulness practice as well. By documenting persistent intrusive thoughts or emotions in one column and countering them with balanced, truthful reflections in another, we begin to reshape our inner dialogue.

Not all emotions need to be reframed—some simply need to be felt. Grief, anger, and sorrow can serve as the bitter medicine that ultimately offers us healing. By fully experiencing our emotions, we allow them to rise, crest, and naturally pass through us, rather than suppressing them, only to have them resurface as pain, anxiety, or even illness. Mindfulness teaches us to sit with these emotions without resistance or judgment, embracing our full humanity as we navigate the otherworldly grief of a Soulmate Addiction healing journey. Much like the urge surfing technique discussed earlier, mindfulness helps us ride the waves of sorrow and longing, honoring our emotions without being consumed by them. In doing so, we discover that even the most intense pain, when given space to be fully felt, eventually softens—reminding us that no feeling is permanent and that healing is always, quietly, unfolding within us.

Like a muscle, mindfulness strengthens with practice. At first, our efforts may feel small, the benefits subtle. But over time, we may notice a shift—the emotional charge surrounding our Soulmate begins to take a different form as the once-consuming, obsessive thoughts lose their grip and the storm within settles. Like a hornet's nest left undisturbed, the mind grows quiet, and in that stillness, we can begin to reclaim our inner peace.

Meditation

Meditation is both a vast and vital subject—one that has inspired countless books, teachings, and personal journeys across centuries. For those new to the practice, a deeper exploration is not only encouraged but often life-changing. While meditation offers profound benefits for all, it holds deep healing power for those navigating emotional pain, grief, or inner turmoil.

Both meditation and mindfulness are forms of mental training that gently guide us away from distorted thinking and obsessive thought patterns. They create a spaciousness within the mind, allowing us to reclaim control over our thoughts—rather than being swept away by the storm of Soulmate Addiction. While mindfulness is rooted in present-moment awareness, meditation is that—and more. We can be mindful without meditating, but true meditation cannot exist without mindfulness.

Research has shown that meditation can change the structure of our brains for a more positive living experience. For instance, a study published in *JAMA Internal Medicine* found that mindfulness meditation can reduce symptoms of anxiety and depression, and another published study found that meditation may help lower blood pressure, which can reduce the risk of heart disease and stroke. Another study published in Psychological Science suggests that just a few minutes of mindfulness meditation can improve attention and working memory. This can lead to better performance in tasks that require focus and concentration. Studies using neuroimaging techniques have found that regular meditation can increase gray matter density in areas of the brain associated with learning, memory, and emotional regulation. This suggests that meditation may have long-term effects on brain health and resilience.

Meditation is a practice that involves training the mind to focus and redirect thoughts. There are many approaches to this, but one of the simplest begins with sitting quietly, closing the eyes, and gently focusing on the breath. With time and patience, the mind grows still. And in that stillness, there comes a moment—perhaps fleeting—when we are completely present, suspended at the sharp, luminous edge of now. Not lost in the past. Not racing toward the future. Just being. In a state of nothingness that somehow holds everything.

There are many rich forms of meditation to explore, each offering unique support on the path of healing. Loving-kindness meditation, mantra meditation, guided visualizations, candle-gazing, and breathwork-based practices can all serve as powerful tools in our journey to transcend and transform the deep emotional ache of Soulmate addiction.

In meditation, we do not escape the self—we return to it, softened and strengthened by presence.

Breathwork/Deep Breathing

Along the lines of mindfulness and meditation (and often incorporated as part of these practices), deep breathing and breathwork are powerful tools to include in our Soulmate Addiction toolbox. Breathwork engages the body's parasympathetic nervous system, triggering a relaxation response that counteracts the physiological effects of stress.

By slowing down and deepening the breath, it is possible to regulate our heart rate, lower our blood pressure, and calm the mind, fostering a greater sense of peace, tranquility, and feelings of empowerment and self-control. Simple techniques such as deep breathing or gentle breath counting become invaluable companions when navigating cravings, allowing us to ride the wave of desire as it rises, crests, and naturally falls away. Beyond these immediate physiological benefits, breathwork serves as a bridge to emotional healing. Whether practiced daily or turned to in times of distress, it creates space for us to access and release stored tension and unprocessed trauma, gently guiding us back to balance.

When a craving for connection with our Soulmate arises, we can pause—sitting or standing comfortably—and bring our awareness to the breath. Closing the eyes, we inhale deeply through the nose, envisioning a radiant, healing light filling the lungs and body. As we exhale slowly through the mouth, we imagine tension, longing, and emotional residue being released.

Maintaining this steady rhythm, we stay present with the sensations in the body, allowing the breath to slow and deepen naturally. As the mind settles, we observe the craving with compassionate detachment, recognizing it as a transient sensation—

not a directive. With each breath, we imagine the urge dissolving, replaced by a grounded sense of strength and inner resolve. We continue breathing in this way until the craving softens, leaving us anchored in a greater sense of calm, control, and empowerment.

Movement

When dealing with our Soulmate Addiction, we spend so much time trying to smile while trying to grieve, and trying to function while falling apart inside, that we often become masters at shoving our emotions deep down inside. An important ingredient in healing trauma is to feel it and let it flow. In our need to hold up the world while it feels like ours is ending, we can often interrupt the flow of our natural grieving process, and this energy can become stuck in our nervous system. As tension builds and residual energy lodges in our body, our vitality is sapped, and our emotional resilience suffers.

Movement can disrupt this process and open the space for healing to occur. In the struggle to conquer our longings and cravings, movement allows for the release of this stagnant energy, clearing away blockages that may hinder our healing and growth, while the endorphins that are released act as natural pain relievers and mood enhancers. Practices such as yoga, tai chi, and qigong integrate movement with mindfulness techniques, offering a holistic approach to addiction recovery by promoting relaxation and self-awareness, and helping to move grief and trauma out of our bodies.

Participating in group exercise, whether through team sports or fitness classes, not only strengthens the body but also nurtures a sense of community, easing feelings of isolation. Even among those who may not fully understand our journey, we can find camaraderie, encouragement, and the quiet reassurance that we are not alone.

A simple walk in nature offers a gentle and deeply healing way to soothe the soul, reconnecting us with the natural world when loneliness and longing for our Soulmate feel overwhelming. Likewise, dancing—whether in solitude or with others—becomes a powerful practice, allowing energy to flow freely and releasing negativity from both body and spirit.

As we move through the healing process of Soulmate Addiction, regular physical movement will prove to be an invaluable ally, seamlessly integrating into our toolbox of self-restoration and renewal.

Energy Work

Reiki, BioGenesis, Healing Touch, acupuncture, massage, and reflexology are all types of energy work modalities whose purpose is to help move "stuck" energy and restore us to our natural state of balance and well-being. Heartbreak is called heartbreak for a reason—it is not just an emotional wound but an energetic one—a pain so intense it can feel as though our very heart is being torn apart. In those moments, we may long for nothing more than for the suffering to end. Yet, heartbreak lingers, and no matter how vigilant we try to be, fragments of that pain embed themselves within our hearts and bodies. Energy work modalities can be incredibly effective in providing relief by shifting blocks that are deeply lodged within us and challenging to remove in any other way.

Prayer and Connection

Regardless of our religion or spiritual beliefs, prayer remains one of the most supportive tools available to us on the journey of Soulmate Addiction. In triple-blind, randomized controlled trials, studies have shown that there are benefits to the use of prayer. Whether we believe in a single, all-powerful deity, a divine oneness, multiple sources of divinity, or nothing at all, prayer has the power to connect us to forces beyond our immediate perception—offering solace, guidance, and a strength that transcends the limits of the mind.

In the depths of pain, longing, loneliness, and even despair, prayer gently reminds us that we do not walk this path alone. Some prayers may bring serenity and healing when spoken aloud or silently in a repetitive manner, while others lend their power to us from the meaning of their words. Whether spoken aloud, whispered in the stillness, or silently carried within, prayer need not follow a prescribed form. Whether we subscribe to more formal wording or create our own invocations—expressions of healing, surrender, or hope call forth the unseen support that is always present, waiting to embrace us.

Ho'oponopono Prayer: (pronounced HO-oh-Pono-Pono) Ho'oponopono is a powerful Hawaiian prayer of forgiveness which roughly translates into "make things right" or "to move back to balance". Directed to our Soulmate, ourselves, our situation, or even a health issue, the Ho'oponopono prayer can provide immediate relief and healing in any number of areas of our life. It is simple, effective, and easy to remember.

While we may find it difficult to direct this prayer to our Soulmate when we believe that we are the injured party, central to this age-old spiritual custom lies the belief in the interconnectedness of all things. What affects one affects the collective and thoughts shape our reality, so the act of pardoning, taking "total responsibility", and harmonizing all areas of our life is a powerful practice for positive change.

To practice the Ho'oponopono prayer, we simply focus our attention on any person or situation we choose, and repeat (internally or aloud) seven to ten times the mantra *"I'm Sorry, Please Forgive Me, Thank you, I love you."* We can repeat this as many times as we wish throughout the day, and remember to include ourselves in the practice. Even though we may have suffered greatly as a result of our Soulmate relationship, when we direct our Ho'oponopono prayers towards our Soulmate in a consistent manner (multiple times a day, every day), the healing energy that starts to return to us can be astonishing

Serenity Prayer: Able to be adapted to any religion or Spiritual belief, the Serenity Prayer reminds us that we are not alone as we walk our path and that we are best served by focusing only on the things that we can control. Spoken throughout the day or when facing challenges, it can provide soothing moments of peace, and bring us back to center when things become challenging. Printing this prayer and placing it in a prominent position can also be a helpful tool: *"God, grant me the serenity to accept the things I cannot change, courage to change the things I can, and wisdom to know the difference."*

Personalized Prayer: Sometimes choosing our own prayers works best. Whether we create our own prayer and say it as a mantra, or talk in a conversational tone to the greater power of our belief system, the healing and assistance is in the connection and intention, not necessarily in finding the perfect words.

Religious Prayers: A great number of the world's population identifies with a religion, and turning toward our foundations of faith and belief can not only help us cope with the pain but also provide guidance and healing on our journey.

Sacred Silence

Sometimes trying to heal while trying to live is the hardest part of the Soulmate Addiction recovery journey. Building Sacred Silence into our day can help us balance the emotional drain of having to live our life while experiencing the internal suffering and healing on our journey. Whether it is fifteen minutes we capture from the day by getting up before anyone else in the household, or a block of time we take when sitting in our car before we go into work or home, having time to just *be* can be an important tool for our emotional well-being as we travel Soulmate Addiction recovery journey.

Simple Daily Practice

When the weight of our journey feels overwhelming, simplicity often holds the greatest power. In our lowest moments, when clarity and strength seem distant, a simple three-step practice—"Next Best Step, Faith, Love"—can guide us forward with grace.

Next Best Step: In our lowest moments, when clarity feels out of reach, all we can do is pause, center ourselves, and connect to the Universal energy. In this stillness, we ask to be shown the next best step. There is no need to force an answer; instead, we release our request into the ethers, trusting that guidance will come in its own time. Sometimes, the response arrives through an unexpected conversation, a sudden insight, or a quiet unfolding over the days ahead. By surrendering the need for immediate answers, we loosen our grip on control and signal to the Universe that we are ready to move forward—one step at a time.

Faith: At this stage, it is often beneficial to reconnect with our faith—our true magic wand. Faith reminds us that we are not meant to carry this burden alone. It shifts our perception, releasing the belief that we must solve everything ourselves, and instead anchors us in the truth that we are held in infinite love, understanding, and support. When we surrender to this knowing, we open ourselves to receiving all that is for our highest and best.

Love: The final step is to send love. Much like the Ho'oponopono Prayer, this practice liberates us from the illusion that we are responsible for another's path, struggles, or choices. As the Buddha wisely said, "May all minds be happy." We cannot control the trials of others, nor can we suffer enough to make someone else happy. When we send love to our Soulmate—or to anyone—we release emotional attachments and dissolve the illusion of control, allowing both ourselves and the recipient to move forward with greater freedom.

Even if we believe our Soulmate to be the source of our pain, sending love can be an incredibly liberating and supportive act. This love, given freely and without expectation, must be released like a gentle wave—unattached to us and without the desire for reciprocation. When done with sincerity, its effects ripple beyond what we can see or measure. And while we may never fully know the impact of this practice, we trust that the Universe will carry it exactly where it is needed. Feel free to do this part of the practice multiple times a day, to anyone we choose, and even to ourselves—past, present, or future.

This three-part practice is simple, yet incredibly profound. In our darkest moments, it's practice can carry us through, step by step, from despair to healing and grace.

Being Open to Divine Guidance

Being open to divine guidance allows us access to an infinite source of wisdom and support. When we ask from a place of openness and faith—without clinging to a specific answer or outcome—we create space for the Universe to respond in ways far beyond our expectations. Through signs, synchronicities, and tangible confirmations, clarity and encouragement can arrive precisely when we need them, illuminating our path in ways both subtle and extraordinary.

While our intuition serves as an internal compass, guiding us with quiet wisdom, there are moments when doubt lingers and the way forward feels unclear. In these times, seeking divine guidance can feel like reaching for a lifeline in a sea of uncertainty—offering solace, direction, and a sense of deeper knowing that transcends the bounds of reason. This guidance is always present, a gentle force ready to support us—if only we ask, believe, and are willing to follow the trail of light laid before us.

When we surrender to this higher wisdom, we enter into a sacred partnership with the Universe—each sign, whisper, and synchronicity becoming part of a divine choreography, guiding us lovingly toward our highest good.

Seek Professional Help

While it may be difficult to find a therapist who fully understands the soul-level impact of these connections, working with a professional trained in addiction can provide valuable guidance. Such therapists can help uncover the emotional wounds or past traumas that fuel our attachment, offering tailored strategies to heal and regain balance.

Therapy is a powerful tool for self-discovery, and when engaged in with commitment, it can bring clarity to destructive patterns, fosters self-awareness, and equip us with healthier coping mechanisms. There are many therapeutic approaches available, each with its own focus and often sharing overlapping techniques. A few of these include: Cognitive Behavioral Therapy (CBT), Dialectical Behavior Therapy (DBT), Eye Movement Desensitization and Reprocessing (EMDR), Somatic Therapy, Internal Family Systems (IFS), Therapy, Gestalt Therapy, and Transpersonal Therapy.

Therapy can offer a safe and supportive space to explore the complexities of Soulmate Addiction, with the right tools and guidance, it can be another pathway to deep healing and lasting transformation.

Awareness of Cognitive Distortions

Cognitive distortions are deeply ingrained, irrational thought patterns that warp our perception of reality, often reinforcing negative emotions and self-defeating beliefs. These distortions act as mental filters, distorting how we interpret situations, ourselves, and others. They are often automatic, occurring without conscious awareness, yet they shape our emotional responses and behaviors in many unfortunately impactful ways. These distorted ways of thinking can intensify our emotional dependence, fuel obsessive behaviors, and prolong our unhealthy attachments.

One common cognitive distortion we may experience with regard to our Soulmate is "catastrophizing", where we may assume the worst possible outcome as we contemplate our options. Our thoughts may tell us *If I leave this person, I will never find love of this magnitude again.* The truth is, we cannot possibly know what the Universe has in store for us, and this fear can lead us to desperate attempts to hold on—even as the situation becomes more and more toxic. In this case, catastrophizing makes the idea of leaving feel overwhelming—believing that a breakup will lead to unbearable loneliness or that we will never recover—rather than recognizing our soul's incredible resilience.

Overgeneralization is another distortion that can cause us great pain on our journey. After experiencing heartbreak with our mate, we might conclude *If this relationship with my Soulmate is over, then maybe I am just incapable of love.* This sweeping belief is deeply flawed and can keep us stuck in patterns of overwhelm and helplessness.

Personalization is another common pitfall, where we may take excessive responsibility for the relationship's dysfunction—blaming ourselves entirely for the toxicity, or believing that if we had just been "better" or "more loving," things would have worked out. Meanwhile, "filtering" can cause us to only focus on the good moments in the relationship—clinging to memories of affection while ignoring patterns of control, emotional neglect, or mistreatment. Similarly, "black-and-white thinking" manifests when our love is seen only in extremes—either perfect and destined or completely ruined. We might think *This is truly my only love, and if they don't feel it is worth fighting for, then I am unworthy of love altogether.* The rigid mindset of black and white thinking prevents us from seeing the complexity and fluidity of our soul's journey.

These distortions can fuel anxiety, depression, and low self-esteem, and may even add to the cycle of our Soulmate Addiction. Distortions create cycles of negative thinking that can feel impossible to escape, but by recognizing and challenging these patterns, we can begin to reframe our thoughts—replacing irrational beliefs with more a balanced, constructive perspective and inner dialogue.

Cognitive Behavioral Tools

Cognitive Behavioral Therapy (CBT) offers a rich array of techniques designed to help individuals recognize and transform unhelpful thought patterns and behaviors. While the guidance of a trained therapist can be invaluable in navigating these tools, many of them are easily accessible and can be practiced independently—some of which have been referenced throughout this chapter under various headings.

One effective technique is *Progressive Muscle Relaxation* (PMR), in which we can learn to systematically tense and relax muscle groups to reduce stress and physical tension, allowing us to better handle the crest of an addiction wave, or cope with feelings of distress.

Another effective tool is the *Rubber Band Technique.* This involves wearing a rubber band on the wrist and gently snapping it when negative thoughts or behaviors arise. This physical sensation serves as a reminder to interrupt the unwanted pattern and immediately replace the negative thought with a positive one. This could involve reciting a mantra, focusing on the breath, or redirecting attention to their surroundings. Over time, the technique helps break automatic negative patterns, promoting conscious choice and behavior change.

Stop Thought Technique is an acronym representing four key steps: *Stop, Take a Breath, Observe*, and *Proceed* Mindfully. Each step plays a crucial role in interrupting automatic responses, fostering self-awareness, and promoting more intentional and effective decision-making. Along those same lines is simply picturing a big red stop sign when an unpleasant or anxious thought arises. This allows our brain to reset its trajectory to a different path.

These are just a few of the many tools offered through CBT—each one a small yet potent ally on the journey of healing and recovery, supporting us in cultivating greater awareness, choice, and emotional resilience.

When We Cannot Cut Off Contact

When situations exist that do not allow us to cut off contact, the path to healing may be more challenging, but it is by no means impossible. Beyond co-parenting obligations, it is essential to be brutally honest with ourselves about what is truly impossible versus what is simply uncomfortable or inconvenient. Sometimes, what we perceive as an immovable barrier is, in reality, a difficult but necessary choice. In such cases, we must ask ourselves: which will bring greater suffering—continuing to see them or enduring the discomfort of change?

For those of us who genuinely must maintain contact, many of the healing tools outlined earlier will still serve as powerful support. The next two tools, however, are designed for these circumstances—offering practical ways to stay grounded and continue healing, even in the midst of ongoing connection.

Reframing. When complete distance isn't possible, emotional distance becomes essential. Reframing is a powerful tool that allows us to take every lingering, idealized thought and replace it with an unvarnished truth. It an effective tool for those of us who—do to family or work considerations—must still see our Soulmate.

Reframing is not about bitterness or cruelty; it is about clarity. It is about breaking the spell. When we catch ourselves reminiscing—admiring their smile, recalling the warmth of their embrace, or noticing how they appear put together as they move through the world—we must immediately counter that thought with reality. The betrayals. The moments of disappointment, the broken promises, the look in their eyes when they were caught in deception. That is the real them. Instead of allowing the pull of connection to our Soulmate to dictate our narrative, we can begin to anchor ourselves in what was undeniably wrong—the narcissistic tendencies we overlooked, the red flags we dismissed, the gaslighting, the manipulation, the lies. The ways in which love was twisted into something uncertain, unsafe, or unkind.

This practice requires deliberate intensity. It is not about fairness or balance—it is about survival. This is a cognitive tool for our healing, not for theirs. We must be unwavering in our commitment to rewriting the narrative, to ensuring that every time nostalgia tries to paint them in a golden light, we replace it with the cold, hard truth that set us on this path of recovery in the first place.

When the ache of longing inevitably returns, we can gently turn our attention to truths we once avoided and focus on how destructive or repellent they actually were: the emotional immaturity, the moments of cruelty, the subtle undermining that quietly chipped away at our peace. Not to harden our hearts, but to keep them aligned with reality. We reflect on the damage left behind—not to dwell in resentment, but to stay grounded in the facts of our experience. Because had they truly loved us in the way we needed and deserved, our path would not have led to this painful parting. Obsession thrives in illusion, but clarity lives in truth—and in choosing truth, we begin to reclaim ourselves.

By shifting our focus from idealization to reality, we reclaim our power. We remind ourselves why this chapter had to end, and we make space for a future where we are no longer bound by the chains of this love.

Pre-paving. Before any necessary interaction, it is wise to pre-pave the moment by setting firm intentions, reminding ourselves to limit contact to the bare minimum required, and have a recovery plan in place for afterward. Using the reframing technique above, revisiting the letter we wrote to ourselves, using positive affirmations, or reaching out to a trusted friend are a few ways that we can recover our equilibrium after a difficult encounter. Most importantly, we need to remember that nothing in this physical world is permanent. Circumstances shift. Children grow up. People relocate. Jobs change. The Universe is always in motion, and in time, we will find relief. Our mind will realign with what is truly best for us, and as we stay the course and trust the process, we will find that freedom eventually arises on the horizon.

"The only lasting beauty is the beauty of the heart." – Rumi

It's important to remember that recovering from a Soulmate Addiction is not a linear journey. There is no perfect roadmap, no step-by-step checklist that guarantees a smooth passage to the other side of healing. Instead, recovery unfolds in its own rhythm—a winding path of progress and setbacks, of days filled with hope and strength, followed by moments of aching nostalgia and despair. Through it all, gentleness matters. Even when it feels as though we are standing still, every effort we make, every tool we embrace, every moment we choose healing over longing, moves us closer to freedom.

One day, without even realizing it, we will have gone an hour, an evening, or an entire day without being lost in our Soulmate Addiction. And then, in time, we will look back and see that we have made it through. That life, in all its beauty and possibility, awaits us beyond the shadow of this addiction.

Will we ever forget them? No. Not a Soulmate. Their presence will always linger somewhere within us—not as an open wound, but as a quiet ember glowing with the energetic memory of what once was. These loves don't end when they leave—they echo, shape, and haunt the spaces we grow into afterward. In time, we may be able to truly embrace that this ending was for the best, and yet still carry them in our hearts, offering silent well wishes from afar.

When we meet again—as we will in the vastness beyond this life—we will have the chance to reflect together. To share stories of choices made, paths taken, and the wisdom gathered along the way. And in that moment, we will understand that every twist, every heartbreak, every moment of growth was always leading us toward our highest good.

For additional resources, please visit SoulmateAddiction.com.

CHAPTER 8

THE POWER OF ETERNAL LOVE: ASCENSION AND SOUL GROWTH THROUGH SOULMATE ADDICTION

The deeper sorrow carves into your being the more joy you can contain. Khalil Gibran

Across cultures and sacred lineages, there exists a concept known as *Divine Madness*—a holy disorientation that occurs when the finite self brushes against the Infinite. The veils between worlds thin, and the soul remembers its origin in the Beloved. Sufi poets call it *ishq-e-haqiqi*—the burning, divine love that sears away illusion and leaves only the raw essence of being.

In the ancient traditions of mystics, saints, and poets, this divine fire was not only welcomed—it was revered. To be undone by love was not a loss but a homecoming. As Rumi wrote, "This longing you feel is the return message of the Beloved calling you back." He did not speak of earthly romance but of the soul's hunger to dissolve into its divine origin. This is not madness in the way the world defines it, but an unraveling that blurs the boundaries between self and Source.

When this experience touches our human lives through the presence of another person—when it wears the face of a Soulmate—it lifts us into the heavens and simultaneously lays us bare. In many ways, when we fall into the depths of Soulmate Addiction we are not merely falling in love—we are falling into the Divine Mystery. Caught between two worlds, the sacred and the human, we know—deeply, viscerally—that this love is not ordinary. It feels transcendent, divine, eternal. And yet, we are often brought to our knees by its earthly complications—its timing, its pain, its impossible contradictions. But it is not a mistake. It is a portal.

The agony itself is not a flaw in the design—it is the design. The soul is not interested in comfort; it is interested in evolution.

Originating in Hindu thought, the term *maya* is the illusion of form and separateness that entices us to identify with the impermanent. We chase what we believe we lack. We suffer when we cannot possess what we love. This is called *dukkha*—the inevitable suffering that comes from desire, attachment, and the mistaken belief in duality.

The yearning, the grief, the heartbreak are thresholds to be crossed that initiate us into transformation. We become alchemists, often without our consent—burning away old identities, refining our hearts in the fire of holy longing. The person we once were can no longer survive within the intensity of this process, and in the depths of our heartbreak, something far more eternal is being born. The very ache that shatters us is the same force that stretches the soul beyond its known edges. Forced into change, we must begin the sacred work of turning pain into wisdom. We learn to hold paradox—to love without possession, to desire without expectation, to release while still caring. It is in this tension between devotion and detachment that our soul evolves. We are not broken and here to fix the story. We are awakening, and we are here to feel it.

Rather than being victims of our Soulmate Addiction, we become co-creators. We are remembering something we chose. Before birth, we entered into sacred contracts with other souls—agreements to catalyze one another's growth, to play the roles of lover, betrayer, redeemer, destroyer, mirror. These roles are not assigned from cruelty but from love. Growth often begins in the wreckage of our broken hearts.

But there is a sacred intelligence in the pain that Soulmate Addiction awakens. Though it may feel senseless, even cruel, it is never without purpose. These bonds arrive not by accident, but by design—summoned by the soul to initiate us into deeper truth. One reason they catalyze such profound growth is that, in the beginning, they invite us to be fully seen. In the gaze of the other, something ancient stirs. We recognize ourselves—not the mask, but the essence—and in that recognition, we begin to lower our guard. The walls that have fortified our hearts across lifetimes begin to soften. Through their presence, we are drawn out into true openness and authenticity. We can let down our shields and show ourselves fully, knowing—on some deep level—that we are safe. We may have traveled countless lifetimes together, accumulating the intimate knowledge that, in their arms, we are protected enough to reveal our truth.

Ironically, the very sense of safety that opens us can also expose what most needs healing. What feels like sanctuary can become the place where our deepest lessons emerge.

Sometimes, what distinguishes a destructive addiction from a sacred journey is our orientation. When our attention remains fixed on the other person, we stay caught in longing, grasping, and the ego's need to secure what feels essential. When we turn inward—toward what the bond is revealing and awakening within us—the experience can begin to transform us.

Ascension is often used to describe a movement into greater consciousness. It is not a withdrawal from life, but a change in how we meet it. Our Soulmate Addiction can be a sacred trigger to this process. It can stir old wounds, karmic patterns, and deeply held beliefs about love, worthiness, and control. Its intensity can strip away the defenses we have relied on, leaving us exposed to truths we may not otherwise have faced.

Yet over time, if we choose awareness over unconscious repetition, something miraculous happens: our identity begins to shift. We are no longer just a person who was hurt, abandoned, or addicted to love. We become a soul in motion—awake, alive, and attuned to our own divine essence.

Carl Jung once said, "The meeting of two personalities is like the contact of two chemical substances: if there is any reaction, both are transformed." Old stories, wounds, and egoic defenses are the dross that begin to melt away. The soul knows that the only way forward is through the fire. Not around it. Not above it. But directly into it. We resist, of course. Who wouldn't? We try to make it work. We obsess, we bargain, we plead with the Universe for a different journey. But eventually, we surrender. Not because we are weak—but because we are being remade.

This is a glimpse into the heart of Divine Madness—not chaos, but the divine clarity gained through the disintegration of everything false. In the sacred intoxication of being touched by something greater than logic or form, we begin to see how much of our suffering stems not from love itself, but from our resistance to what it is asking of us. We want to hold on, to possess, to control. But the soul has other plans.

Obsession says, *I need you to complete me.* Devotion says, *Through loving you, I have discovered parts of myself I never knew existed.* Obsession clings. Devotion surrenders. Obsession demands a specific outcome. Devotion allows love to flow in its highest form—even if that means letting go.

In the depths of the longing, the soul begins to whisper its true purpose: this connection exists not just to love another but to remember ourselves. The pain demands we slow down, reflect on old patterns, and face what we have numbed or avoided. It calls us into presence, and through that presence, it returns us to ourselves. Soulmate Addiction is not a detour from our path—it is our path. A winding, holy road where the soul remembers itself through the mirror of another. In their presence, we see not only the beloved—but ourselves, unmasked and magnified. This is the sacred madness of the soul in love—not broken, but breaking open. Not lost, but being found. Again, and again, and again.

Soulmate love is a current, not a container. It cannot be trapped or defined. It flows through and with us, shaping us as it goes. The more we try to grasp it, the more it slips away. But when we surrender to its flow and accept the growth it demands, our rebirth begins. For we are not truly addicted to our Soulmate—we are addicted to the light they have activated within us. And the true work is to claim that light as our own.

This inner shift is not easy. It may require us to die to the version of ourselves that was built around the need for union. We may find ourselves grieving not only the loss of the person, but the loss of the story we attached to them. In the ashes of that grief, something new can be born: self-realization. Pema Chödrön said "Nothing ever goes away until it has taught us what we need to know". Growth and comfort seldom exist in the same space.

As this awakening unfolds, the contours of our inner and outer worlds begin to shift—sometimes so dramatically that even those closest to us may no longer recognize who we are becoming. The pull toward noise, distraction, and stimulation begins to lose its hold. Crowds feel overwhelming. Conflict feels jarring. We may find ourselves inexplicably drawn to silence, stillness, and solitude. The endless chase for achievement, recognition, or relevance in conventional spaces begins to feel hollow. Sensational headlines, heated debates, the drive to compete or to "win"—these begin to feel like echoes from a world that no longer fits.

The spaces that once felt like home—offices buzzing with ambition, dinner parties filled with surface-level chatter—begin to feel foreign, even illusory. Conversations without depth become difficult to endure. We may be called "changed" or dismissed as "boring." But in truth, we are not fading—we are emerging. The old world begins to fall away, revealing the shimmering presence of something more true.

And as the veil lifts, shifts begin to ripple through every aspect of our lives. Friendships that were sustained by routine or resignation dissolve. People leave partnerships they should have left long ago. Jobs that once provided status or security are abandoned in search of meaning. Some move across the country—or across the world—answering an inner summons they can no longer ignore. The soul begins to hunger for depth, for beauty, for truth. The outer world no longer drives us; the inner world becomes the terrain we long to explore.

We discover that joy is not found in the climb, but in the stillness between steps. Creation calls louder than consumption. And from that inner sanctuary of mystery and peace, new manifestations arise—careers that align with our calling, relationships that reflect our wholeness, ways of living that feel more like poetry in motion. The pursuit of more gives way to the presence of enough. We begin to live not from ambition, but from inspiration.

This doesn't mean we abandon all life and responsibility. On the contrary, this awakening often frees us to finally begin the life we were always meant to live. We may write the book that has long whispered through our dreams, start the business that feels like a sacred offering, or step into a version of success that feels rooted, honest, and expansive. We begin asking for the life that reflects our soul—not the life we've curated to meet the expectations of others.

This is the pivot: from obsession to devotion. And this is where the soul work begins. The longing that once seemed centered on the other reveals itself for what it truly is: a longing for the divine within ourselves, stirred awake by love's reflection in another. That unbearable ache was never just for them—it was a call to come home.

The awakening born through Soulmate Addiction may be disorienting, even devastating—but its trajectory is always upward. While ordinary obsessions drag us down—marked by jealousy, insecurity, and control—the transformative love that flows from genuine giving, respect, and a desire for the other's highest good leads us toward expansion and freedom. The sacred fire of a Soulmate connection, when surrendered to, becomes a force that helps to refine us. The intensity that once felt like torment becomes a divine pressure—pushing us not just toward union with another, but toward union with the highest truth of who we are. This is the final gift of Soulmate Addiction—it delivers us back to ourselves. Raw, radiant, and real. No longer seeking salvation in another, we become our own sanctuary.

Eventually, the intensity of this journey softens. The waves of pain subside. What once felt like chaos reveals itself as a sacred design. In the place of torment, we are left with something deeper—a knowing. A wisdom that cannot be taught, only lived. We begin to see the brilliance in the breaking, the clarity in the confusion, the divine choreography beneath the collapse. The heartache becomes initiation. The rupture becomes revelation. We find ourselves changed—not in spite of the love, but because of it.

Through this sacred alchemy, karma becomes purpose. The energy we once hurled outward in longing or blame now turns inward, becoming fuel for healing, creativity, service, and awareness. The obsession does not vanish—it transmutes. What once clung in desperation now opens in devotion. We hold love more lightly, but more powerfully as well. We no longer require it to look a certain way, because we have become the source of what we once sought.

A common myth whispers that Soulmate love must end in union—a lifelong romance that completes the story, heals every wound, and fulfills every longing. But for many, that is not the path. And if we are honest, it was never the point. The Soulmate connection is not about possession or permanence in the physical world; it is about communion—with the self, with spirit, and with the truth of who we are. We are being led into divine remembrance. We are being called into sacred intimacy—with ourselves. And whether or not the other remains in our lives, this shift within us becomes irreversible. The connection may or may not take shape in the physical world. But its deeper purpose is always energetic, always evolutionary.

We begin to gather the scattered fragments of ourselves. We reclaim the hidden pieces, the disowned parts, the buried truths. We anchor into a love no longer dependent on another's gaze, but rooted in the Divine within. We become the lover and the beloved, the seeker and the found. We no longer need the mirror to know who we are. And one day, almost quietly, we notice that the ache for union with our Soulmate has softened. Not because the love has died, but because we have come alive. The bond may remain—but the obsession relinquishes its hold. The pain ripens into wisdom. The lessons bloom.

As the poet Ghalib wrote, "It is through love that the soul has tasted the essence of life." And in that tasting, something unexpected unfolds. The cracks left by loss become passageways for light. Our grief deepens into compassion. Our sensitivity sharpens into intuition. Love expands beyond its original object, radiating through us and toward all beings. For some, the addiction refines into devotion and partnership. For others, the lost beloved may temporarily return. And for still others, they do not. Yet the most essential reunion—the only one that ever truly mattered—is the one that occurs within. We come home to ourselves. And in doing so, we become vessels of a love no longer dependent on outcome to be complete.

As shared earlier in this book, Indra's Web reflects the infinite tapestry of existence—each knot holding a radiant jewel, every jewel mirroring all others in perfect interconnection. In this cosmic design, each soul's awakening sends ripples across the whole. Every healing, every insight, every step forward becomes a glimmer in the greater net, guiding others in turn. Just as our journey through Soulmate Addiction transforms us, it also reflects back into the collective, offering light to others on their path. Our private evolution becomes a shared illumination.

Healing from Soulmate Addiction is not about forgetting or cutting cords—it is about integrating. It is about taking the sacred fire of that love and allowing it to forge something true and lasting in the heart. As the Bhagavad Gita teaches: "No effort on the path of love is ever wasted." We do not return to who we were before—because that version of us has dissolved. In its place stands something deeper, wiser, more whole. Though we may still carry the memory, still feel the echo of that pain within, we are no longer ruled by it. Our soul now steers the course—toward more light, more truth, more becoming.

Those who walk through this Divine Madness do not emerge unscathed. They emerge transformed. Not as untouchable mystics high upon distant peaks, but as embodied souls walking this world with open hearts and softened eyes. We become mystics of the ordinary—able to sit with mystery, to offer presence without needing answers, to see the holy in the mundane, and the Divine in a stranger's gaze.

The Universe, in its infinite wisdom, does not use love only to bring people together—but to bring souls home to themselves. That is the deeper purpose of the Soulmate bond. Whether our journey leads us back into the arms of the one who awakened us, or onward toward new and different forms of love, the gift has already been given. It lives in our decision to become whole—regardless of who stayed or who walked away. We have been undone, yes—but also re-formed. We are not merely survivors of love's fire; we are its alchemists.

In choosing wholeness—whether in union or in solitude—we begin the greatest love story of all: the one where we finally belong to ourselves. We are awakened. We are altered. We are more alive than we ever were before.

And so, as the next chapter of our life unfolds, we may find that our deep inner growth continues. We carry it whether we walk alone or hand in hand with the one who sparked it all. Once the soul awakens, it cannot go back to sleep. And once awake—there is where the real relationship begins. The one with ourselves. The one with life. The one with love. We may choose to love again—not from need, but from fullness. We may follow a new path—not because we are escaping, but because we are answering a deeper call. The journey of Soulmate Addiction doesn't end—it integrates. It becomes a golden thread woven into the fabric of our becoming.

We no longer see the experience as a wound to be healed, but as a rite of passage. A sacred unraveling that revealed the truth of our being. We loved. We longed. We broke. We grew.

And we emerged—whole.

Now let's move forward—not in longing, but in presence—as we explore how to hold both fire and stillness in a soul-connected bond.

CHAPTER 9

MINDFUL SOULMATE CONNECTIONS: BALANCING PASSION AND PEACE

Life is a balance of holding on and letting go. Rumi

Celeste lifted her gaze to the silent moon as it climbed above the dark, unmoving treetops. The cool night air kissed her skin, a sharp contrast to the fire's molten glow, its flickering light mirroring the quiet flame within her heart. She turned toward the man beside her, knowing this moment was not just a fleeting spark but the culmination of a long, winding journey. She marveled at all that had come before—babies born, houses built, careers attended to, and lives broken and mended to rise again. Every thread of their past woven into the tapestry of the now. The days of angst were finally gone; their love had birthed into so much more than she could have ever hoped for. Few ever arrived at such a place, and Celeste knew how fortunate she was.

From the moment she first met Ryan, he had captured her soul's attention, awakening longings she hadn't known existed and igniting a love that refused to fade through the following years spent apart. Life in their physical worlds may have kept them separated, but her heart and soul somehow remained a part of his as they continued with obligations that bound them elsewhere. They spent years as long-distance friends—their connection an ember that refused to die—and yet, they also loved with loyalty and determination those they had chosen first. In that way, their story remained suspended between fidelity, longing, and the unanswered claims of the heart.

Her mind drifted back to those years of quiet suffering, to the nights spent wrestling with the agony of longing. How many nights had she lain awake, divided between loyalty and desire? She remembered hearing his name in passing conversation and feeling the ache of unclaimed love. She recalled sitting at a concert beside a man who rarely gave her a moment's notice, wishing with every fiber of her being that it was Ryan's hand resting in hers as she watched the players on the stage. She had never intended to shatter her marriage. It was Brodie who set her free, his years of infidelity finally surfacing like wreckage from deep waters. She knew she should have felt pain and betrayal—but all she felt was liberation.

Ryan's road had been crueler. His was a slow descent into despair as his partner dismantled their life together—one painful choice at a time. He knew that Ava's refusal to confront the wounds of her past was at the core of her emotional volatility, her cycles of blame, withdrawal, and destruction. But he also understood, with increasing clarity, that he could not mend what he did not break. Her inner world was a locked chamber he had never been permitted to enter, and in truth, he realized he had only ever been standing at the threshold.

So he helplessly reacted to each crisis without ever being able to get ahead of any of them. They arrived without notice and, each time took a piece of his heart, mind, and financial landscape. From discovering maxed out credit cards, to finding a neighbor on his doorstep threatening legal action, Ryan never knew what disaster would land next. He had fought for her—for the life he had tried so hard to preserve—but in the end, he couldn't protect even himself from the wreckage she left behind.

So, at last, he had walked away.

After that, only one truth remained—to deny that his love for Celeste remained alive through all of these years would be the greatest mistake of all. And now, here they were. Not as two people desperately clinging to love, but as two souls who had weathered life's tempests and emerged, at last, into the quiet glow of something enduring. The fire crackled, the moon rose higher, and they both knew—with a certainty deeper than words—that this moment was not the end of their story. It was only the beginning.

Whatever our souls are made of, his and mine are the same. Emily Brontë

It's our heart's greatest desire that we live happily ever after with our Soulmate, and the Universe can be our greatest co-conspirator. Our souls crave the exhilaration of reunion, while our hearts seek the quiet constancy of presence, peace, and love; Destiny weaves these threads of possibility together for the grand design of our lives. Ryan and Celeste had discovered the rarest of gifts—what becomes possible when two souls find their home in each other's arms. For these two, the path was one of assimilating great longing and love into a mosaic of tender, beautiful moments stretched out over the decades of life together. These Soulmates found wholeness within their relationship because they had found it within themselves first, and this love would serve as the foundation as they built and lived the life of their dreams. There was no longing for change, no soul crying for more. Just the tick-tock beating of two hearts finally at one with one another.

In contrast, such happily ever after stories can be challenging for some Soulmate couples to write. Once the addictive qualities of a Soulmate connection are slated with the reunification of finding their home in each other, whatever lay hidden beneath may be freed from the shadows and rise to the surface in ways we could not have anticipated.

Emily and James met through a mutual friend, and from the very first glance, their connection was electric, instant, undeniable, and all-consuming. It was as if their souls had recognized each other before their minds had could catch up, and from that moment on, an invisible force bound them together, shaping their every thought and decision.

Petite and effortlessly graceful, Emily was known among her friends for her pragmatism—her steady nature a grounding force in the lives of those around her. James, in contrast, was a dreamer—restless, untamed, and drawn to the unknown. Together, they were a breathtaking pair, their differences not a source of conflict but rather the fire that fueled their fascination with each other. Each knew, without question, that they had found their cosmic counterpart, and the "completion" factor of their partnership reinforced their growing Soulmate Addiction. Their love became both an elixir and a poison, an exquisite prison they had no desire to escape. The outside world faded into insignificance, as dreams they once held close slipped through their fingers, abandoned in favor of the only thing that truly mattered—each other. Separation, even for a moment, was agony. Reuniting was ecstasy. Their lives fused into one seamless existence, where nothing and no one else could intrude. Friends and family watched with growing concern as Emily and James drifted further from their responsibilities and relationships, their well-being sacrificed at the altar of their love.

Emily was the first to finally notice and question whether the closeness of their unworldly bond was sustainable. When her mother sent her an article on love addiction, she had initially dismissed it with anger—after all, how could anyone who had never felt such a connection as theirs possibly understand? But as the days and weeks had passed, the unsettling realization took root: she longed for balance. She missed the pieces of herself she had left behind, and in her heart of hearts, she knew that she and James could have both each other and a wonderful, well-rounded life together.

James, however, seemed to need only her. Co-dependency. Trauma bonding. Attachment wounds. Unresolved childhood scars. Beneath the surface of their all-encompassing love, James's shadows threatened to drown them with chains of dysfunction and pain. The depths of their connection had awakened something buried within him, something far more devastating than even he had realized. The loss of his mother in childhood had left wounds that had never fully healed—abandonment fears wrapped in layers of quiet resilience. For years, he had concealed his grief behind a mask of strength, upholding it for his father's sake, terrified that if he faltered, he would lose him too. And now, to love Emily— whose life still held the warmth and safety of a mother's love—was to awaken a five-year-old boy's silent devastation. The echoes of his childhood loss reverberated through their love, turning his need for her into something far greater than romance. She was not just his partner—she was the air he breathed, the anchor he had long sought.

So, as Emily began to find space and reclaim fragments of the world outside their love, James clung tighter. His need for her was visceral, his longing sharpening into desperation. To him, it became more than love—it was survival. Their love had begun as a cosmic reunion written in the stars. But now, it threatened to unravel them entirely.

"To lose balance sometimes for love is part of living a balanced life." In Elizabeth Gilbert's *Eat, Pray, Love,* the author talks to a guru who reassures her that sometimes it is okay to go all out and lose our balance for a time. Diving deep into love IS part of the human experience. At times, we crave the contrast between where we are—searching, yearning, feeling alone—and the exhilarating fulfillment of finally discovering the connection we've longed for. The sheer beauty of it can momentarily sweep us into the enchanting spell of limerence, where the world feels brighter, the grass greener, and the sun warmer. In that euphoria, we surrender to the intoxicating bliss of our Soulmate love bubble. Like Emily and James, we may find ourselves pausing in life, captivated by the profound reunion of our souls and the feeling of finally coming home. With all the intensity this stage brings, a touch of Soulmate Addiction is almost inevitable.

For James, however, his addiction to Emily had awakened deep, unresolved parts of himself, making life with her unsustainable in its current form. Fortunately, their love held strong, and he was eventually willing to face the difficult work of uncovering the hidden rivers of pain running beneath his solid exterior. Years of therapy, holistic practices, and deep inner work became his commitment—not just to himself, but to the life he was committed to having with Emily. Through this journey, they discovered a delicate balance—one that allowed their souls to remain deeply connected while also growing in their own, necessary ways.

As a fulfilled individual, we bring more to a partnership than someone who relies solely on their partner for happiness. Maintaining a sense of self allows for the greatest chance at long-term success within a relationship of such great soul connection. Now, years later, James could still gaze at Emily in awe. Where once the mere thought of losing her would have sent him spiraling into desperate insecurity, he now met such fears with a quiet acceptance and certainty. He understood that love, by its very nature, carried the potential for loss. Yet, rather than clinging in fear, he found peace in the knowledge that their bond was eternal—something that could never be possessed, only honored and revered.

The transition from Soulmate Addiction to a balanced, fulfilling love can be a challenging but worthwhile journey. Calling in our Soulmate may feel like the greatest accomplishment of our lifetime, yet the true test begins once that dream is realized. As the euphoria of reunion settles, we must find our footing in order to stand in our happily ever after. From there, love becomes less about intensity and more about intention—woven through the everyday moments that build a real and lasting Soulmate experience.

The only lasting beauty is the beauty of the heart. Rumi

Transitioning from a life shaped by longing, anticipation, and emotional intensity to one of peace and deep connection can feel unexpectedly disorienting. When our days have been shaped by longing and the exhilarating pursuit of love, the quiet certainty of Soulmate reunification may feel strangely unfamiliar. We may even find ourselves fearing the future, wondering: Can it possibly get better than this?

As our soul begins to rest in the steady presence of our beloved, our ego may stir, whispering that something is missing. The ache of desire, the endless striving—releasing this emotional current can leave us feeling oddly untethered. It is often said that safety can feel like danger when we are unaccustomed to it. A soul conditioned to chase may feel strangely unmoored in the presence of what it has long sought. When absence has been our compass, the fullness of love's arrival can feel almost… wrong. Too easy. Too still.

In this delicate stage of Soulmate reunification, self-awareness becomes essential. The mind and nervous system, long attuned to the chase, may struggle to trust the calm. In our discomfort, we might unconsciously project our inner discomfort onto our Soulmate or the relationship itself, searching for an external cause when the disturbance is actually arising within. For some, time is enough to smooth these edges, bringing a quiet reassurance to the unsettled soul. For others, finding the balance between passion and peace requires a deeper commitment to inner work.

Over time, we begin to adjust to our Soulmate's presence. As the intensity of reunion settles and daily life reasserts itself, the relationship must make room for smaller frustrations—damp laundry left in the washer, the sting of feeling unheard, the minor disappointments and mismatches that come with ordinary life. The brilliant radiance of reunion may no longer eclipse every inconvenience. And in a tired, unguarded moment, we may find ourselves looking at the person we once longed for with a quiet and disorienting question: *Where did the magic go?*

For some, this is dangerous new territory. As the once-intoxicating highs of Soulmate Addiction give way to a steadier emotional landscape, those with more addictive tendencies may struggle to adapt. The chemistry of eternal love shifts—from an electrifying rush to a deeper, more enduring intimacy. The rush of pursuit no longer floods the system with the same euphoria or shields us from the frustrations of ordinary life. For anyone who depended on that intensity to escape the mundane, its fading can feel like a profound loss.

For these individuals, the path forward may require sustained effort. Tools such as those in Chapter 7 must become part of a long-term practice of self-care, much like a person recovering from any addiction. Just as those healing from substance dependency often benefit from ongoing support, those deeply entangled in Soulmate Addiction may find solace in therapy or a like-minded community. Yet, having an addictive personality does not mean the Soulmate journey must end. If the Soulmate relationship is otherwise healthy, a compassionate partner can hold space for their beloved's struggles, walking alongside them as they navigate the winding road toward balance. As Ram Dass once said, "We are all walking each other home." For some, the path can be a bit more winding.

For those less influenced by addictive tendencies, this transition can still pose challenges. Fortunately, our biology supports us in this phase. As our hearts adjust to the sweet cadence of daily Soulmate connection, our brains undergo a transformation. The love hormone oxytocin deepens our sense of security, calmness, and contentment. Meanwhile, its chemical cousin, vasopressin, fortifies monogamous commitment, reinforcing the "tend and defend" instinct that binds couples together through life's challenges. These non-romantic aspects of Soulmate Addiction work to solidify our connection even in the face of the demands and dramas of physical life.

Unlike the instinct-driven regions that once fueled the intoxicating highs of Soulmate Addiction, long-term love engages cognitive areas responsible for reasoning, reward-based learning, and adaptive function—while still preserving the deeper mechanisms of attachment. Over time, as we exercise patience with ourselves and each other, the neural circuits that cultivate bonding and security take precedence, even as the dopamine-fueled euphoria of early passion settles into a steadier, more sustainable rhythm.

"You could say that love begins as a stressor, but then love becomes a buffer against stress," explains Thomas Sherman, Professor at Georgetown School of Medicine. The fiery passion, the emotional extremes, and the intoxicating highs of early love eventually soften as the brain's chemistry stabilizes. The once-relentless craving is replaced by something sweeter: a quiet security and a steadfast presence that shields us from life's inevitable upheavals. Much of this can sound very non-romantic, but this is where the real love story begins. Not in the fevered chase, nor in the excruciating longing, but in the quiet, intentional choosing. Again and again.

Love doesn't just sit there, like a stone, it has to be made, like bread; remade all the time, made new. Ursula Le Guin, *The Lathe of Heaven.*

Though even Soulmate love calls for continued commitment as we move through the seasons of life, the magic of our experience need not fade with time. In a groundbreaking study conducted at Stony Brook University, researchers Bianca Acevedo, Ph.D., and Arthur Aron, Ph.D., explored the brain activity of individuals who had been married for an average of 21 years, comparing them to those in the early stages of romantic infatuation. Using MRI scans, the team observed the brains of participants who reported being deeply in love with their spouse, even after decades together. Remarkably, the scans revealed that the same neural regions associated with reward and desire—the "wanting" that fuels new love—were still highly active in these long-term couples. As Dr. Richard Schwartz of Harvard Medical School noted, "A state-of-the-art investigation of love has confirmed for the very first time that people are not lying when they say that after 10 to 30 years of marriage, *they are still madly in love with their partners*."

Perhaps even more fascinating was another discovery: the neural activity of those in long-term, passionate relationships bore similarities to that of individuals experiencing a cocaine-induced high. This supports the idea that the state of being in love—no matter for how long—can share many of the same properties as addiction.

Science affirms what the soul has always known: true love does not diminish—it evolves.

Can people enter a relationship with their Soulmate and not fall into some level of addiction to them? The answer is yes—it's possible, though certainly not the most common scenario. Love, in its purest form, transcends addiction, and we are not just souls—we are complex beings shaped by our personalities, appearances, genetics, and the echoes of our earliest wounds. Sometimes, our Soulmate arrives in an unexpected form—a name that feels foreign on our tongue, a crooked smile, a body that doesn't match our usual desires. They may carry a trace of arrogance, lack the social grace we're drawn to, or come from a family dynamic that unsettles us. And yet, beyond these earthly facades, our souls recognize something timeless—something real.

We may hesitate, stumble through the early stages, unsure of what exactly we've found. And still, their presence lingers in our thoughts. We return to them, even when logic protests. We feel them, even in their absence. The soul knows.

In today's world, it's rare to hear someone say, "This life will not be long enough to love my partner." Yet there are couples who move through the world in quiet synchronicity—finishing each other's sentences, weaving through the kitchen with unspoken rhythm, intuitively sensing when to lean in and when to let go. Over time, the rhythm of their bond deepens into something both grounding and transcendent—the very essence of what we imagine love could be. As neuroscientist Dr. Stephanie Cacioppo, author of *Wired for Love*, explains: "People in love have this symbiotic, synergistic connection thanks to the mirror neuron system, and that's why we often say some couples are better together than the sum of their parts."

The secret to a lasting, harmonious Soulmate relationship lies in the delicate balance between passion and peace, between the intensity of the heart and the serenity of the soul. Love, like nature, requires balance. To nurture this journey, we must first understand our soul's deepest needs and allow the space for them to manifest.

With patience, self-awareness, and a willingness to walk this path with open hearts, the early stages of Soulmate reunification become fertile ground from which lasting love can take root. But love, like anything alive, must be nurtured with care. A plant that grows too quickly from over watering may appear lush at first, but without the grounding of sun, wind, and time, it may not survive the storms to come. In the same way, relationships that rush headlong into intimacy—fueled by intensity but lacking in clarity—can develop quiet fractures beneath the surface. It is not enough to merge souls; we must also understand the human beings behind them. To build something enduring, we must be willing to tend to what arises—old wounds, inherited patterns, unconscious habits—and gently release what no longer serves. When love is given room to breathe, and when both partners commit to growth alongside connection, the bond is no longer fragile—it becomes rooted, resilient, and real. Soulmate love is not a single moment of recognition, but a living, evolving dance: one that honors the soul, while choosing the person, again and again.

So, whether love stands present or waits on the horizon, the journey remains the same: becoming capable of holding great love with grace. This path calls for sacred resilience, the willingness to evolve, and the courage to meet both light and shadow within. It is then that love can transform beyond Soulmate Addiction into a lasting presence—a steady flame that endures through all seasons.

CONCLUSION

THE JOURNEY HOME

"You've seen my descent, now watch my rising." Rumi

Soulmates and Twin Flames etch the greatest chapters ever written on our hearts: Fate sets the stage, synchronicity drops breadcrumbs, and karma cues the lights, as two souls step into scenes of force and folly, heartbreak and ecstasy, malady and miracle. Whether our Soulmates or Twins arrive as protagonist, foil, or unexpected villain, their presence leaves an imprint no other soul can quite erase. Their arrival marks a pivotal turn in the soul's story—one that forever alters the life it touches.

These stories do not always follow the logic of the world. They unfold in a different realm, where lifetimes echo, recognition is immediate, and the heart remembers what the mind cannot explain. And yet, these meetings between the Divine and the human are not always seamless. Our spiritual nature may recognize the harmony of the bond, while our human wiring struggles to contain its force. When the chemistry of the body collides with the timelessness of a Soulmate connection, everything can go into overdrive. Boundaries blur. Body, mind, and spirit light up. The result can be an intensity so powerful it seems to exceed ordinary love—like being set on fire from the inside out.

For some, this fiery bond evolves into a deep and balanced partnership—love that is both mystical and grounded, divine and durable. But for others, especially where trauma, unhealed wounds, or conflicting paths are involved, the connection becomes entangled with addiction. The Soulmate who awakens us may also be the one who destabilizes us. And in that contradiction lies the addictive pull: the ecstasy of reunion, the agony of absence, the ache for a love that feels like oxygen—essential, elusive, and beyond control.

But the soul is wise—it waits, even as we spin. It holds steady beneath the chaos. And eventually, something within us begins to shift. Over time, the pain of holding on becomes greater than the pain of letting go. It is here that the longing for peace begins to turn the tide, and a new story quietly emerges. We reach for support, for healing, for guidance—and slowly, another way becomes possible. As time and reflection do their quiet work, we come to understand that pain does not have to define the end of our story. We begin to see that it is possible to live from fullness rather than from loss and longing.

In time—and with intention—the ache gives way to growth. What once felt like fate becomes fuel for transformation. The intensity that once consumed us begins to reveal its deeper purpose: awakening. Soulmate Addiction, for all its fire and confusion, is not the end. It can become an initiation into deeper self-knowledge. Not all Soulmates remain. Not all Twin Flames walk beside us in the physical realm. Some serve their role in a single act before the curtain falls. But even their departure leaves its mark, their presence forever etched into the architecture of the soul.

The true alchemy begins when the story turns inward—when the soul begins to seek not reunion with another, but reunion with itself. This is where healing begins.

With every step away from the chaos of craving, we move closer to the wisdom of our soul. We learn that not every love story ends in union—and not every union serves the soul. We begin to see the deeper design: that the connection was never solely about the other person. It was about our evolution. It was about waking up.

And that awakening—painful though it may be—is the great gift of Soulmate Addiction. It asks us to confront both the shadow and the sacred. It asks us to release illusion, loosen attachment, and return to the center within. From this place of clarity and integration, the next act of life begins to unfold—not from addiction or seeking, but from being. We no longer yearn from emptiness. We create from wholeness. We begin to attract relationships rooted in resonance, not need.

Some Soulmates stay. Some return. Others do not. Some stories rekindle in healthier ways. Others dissolve like mist. And if love comes again, it does not arrive to rescue us—but to walk beside us. Regardless of the outcome, something essential within us has changed. Old patterns fall away. We stop searching for a savior—we become our own sanctuary. We no longer chase a mirror—we embody the love, worth, and truth we once sought in another. We tend to our wounds. We release the need to measure our value by someone else's presence or absence. We soften. We expand. And gradually, we rise into the version of ourselves that this love was always meant to reveal.

Solitude may become a sacred companion, allowing the soul to rest in its own radiant presence. Wherever the path leads, the soul knows. Resonance will always find resonance. What aligns will remain. We find peace not in avoiding the silence, but in trusting the soul's timing.

And so, the story continues—not with addiction, but with ascension. Not with craving, but with clarity. The next act is written by a soul no longer seeking from lack, but offering from fullness. From this space, new partnerships may form—ones built on mutual recognition, shared wholeness, and grace. Through these eternal connections, the soul is not broken but broken open.

For love, at its highest, returns the soul to its own light.

ABOUT AUTHOR

Judith Hartke is the author of *Soulmate Addiction: The Power and Peril of Love's Eternal Bond.* An artist, intuitive, medium, and teacher, her work explores the intersection of emotional attachment, personal transformation, and spiritual growth. Drawing from decades of spiritual practice, creative work, and private client experience, she writes about the powerful bonds that shape us, awaken us, and challenge us to grow. Judith holds a B.S. from Cornell University and has taught nearly 2,000 classes in metaphysical studies, including at Lily Dale Assembly in New York. Learn more at JudithHartke.com and SoulmateAddiction.com.

NOTES

If this book moved or supported you in any way, please consider leaving a review on Amazon. Your words help other readers discover it, and I am deeply grateful for each one.

Now available: *The Soulmate Addiction Recovery Workbook*, a companion workbook with practical tools for healing addictive relationship patterns.

Coming soon: *My Soulmate Story:* A Guided Keepsake Journal for Your Soulmate Journey.

Please visit *SoulmateAddiction.com* to learn more and join the mailing list for future updates.

With gratitude,

Judith Hartke

www.ingramcontent.com/pod-product-compliance
Lightning Source LLC
LaVergne TN
LVHW020627100826
845148LV00012B/2086

* 9 7 9 8 2 1 8 7 1 5 3 4 2 *